WOMAN'S OWN
Family Garden

WOMAN'S OWN

Family Garden

Jennifer Curry

Hamlyn
London · New York · Sydney · Toronto

Dedication
For my Mother and Father who love their garden

Acknowledgements
Line artwork by Robert Micklewright
Line artwork on pages 26 and 27 only by Norman Barber
Colour artwork on pages 102 and 103 by John Rignall

The publishers would like to thank Cramphorn Ltd. of
Chelmsford for supplying garden furniture and tools for
photographic purposes.
Thanks are also due to Mr. R. H. M. Robinson of
The Harry Smith Horticultural Photographic Collection, and
members of his family and staff who assisted at photographic
sessions, and to *Amateur Gardening*, Pat Brindley, Robert
Corbin, John Cowley, Bryan Dunn, Anthony Huxley and
Elsa Megson for supplying colour and black and white
photographs.

First published in 1978 by
The Hamlyn Publishing Group Limited
London · New York · Sydney · Toronto
Astronaut House, Feltham, Middlesex

Filmset in England by Tradespools Limited, Frome, Somerset
in 10 on 12pt. Monophoto Plantin.
Printed and bound in England by Cox and Wyman Limited, Fakenham

Contents

Introduction 10

Before You Start 12

Getting to Know Your Garden 14

Planning for Pleasure 28
The Starter Garden 30
The Nursery Garden 38
The Growing-up Garden 48
The Growing-old Garden 54

Gardens, New and Old 62

Making the Most of a Small Plot 70

What Plants to Grow

A Herb Garden 80

A Kitchen Garden 84
A Few Fruits 90

Some Specialities
Roses for Every Garden 94
Birds in the Garden 102
A Butterfly Sanctuary 108
Planting for Fragrance 110
A Winter Border 114
A White Garden 116

The Labour-free Garden 120

Index 122

Introduction

There comes a time, for most of us, when we find ourselves the owners of a garden.

Gardens come in all sorts of shapes and sizes. You may find yourself with a couple of window-boxes on a sky-high balcony . . . a concrete back-yard . . . a basement area . . . quarter of an acre of ancient orchard . . . or a raw patch of earth surrounding a brand-new house. But no matter how large or small it is, no matter how old or new, no matter whether it is shaded or sun-splashed, damp or dry, every garden has this in common – it is an extension of your living space. You can make it an invaluable part of your home life with something to offer all the family, from toddlers to teenagers, from newly weds to Darby and Joan.

Your garden is so much more than a view from your window. It can be a place to sit and relax, or to work; a place to eat and drink, or entertain your friends. It can be a playground for the children, a party-room for the teenagers. It can provide the family not only with food and flowers, but also with drinks and decorations, cosmetics and confections, rinses and remedies, perfumes, pot-pourris, potions and presents.

All you need is a little bit of time, a little bit of money, and a whole lot of bright ideas – and you may be surprised how much fun you will get from it.

Below: A garden can be either large and spacious, incorporating several areas with different moods and functions or a simply paved basement area and steps as shown opposite.

Before You Start

Be prepared. You will need a few items of basic equipment which will make your tasks much easier. However, don't be alarmed. Most gardening books give you such a frighteningly comprehensive list of 'essential' tools in Chapter 1 that you can't even afford to read Chapter 2. This book is different. Few of us have the money or storage space for a vast array of garden tools, especially since many of them can be done without perfectly easily.

Essential Tools
Those that I have found I *can't* do without are a trowel, which is, without doubt, my most-used tool, a spade, a fork, sharp secateurs, a Dutch hoe, a rake and a lightweight watering can.

These, among them, will cope with the vast majority of garden chores, but if you have a lawn you will also need a mower, powered, if possible.

Most of these can be kept neatly stored, in the minimum of space, held upright against a wall in the shed or garage by large spring clips.

Finally, a barrow, narrow enough to negotiate garden paths and sensibly designed for simple emptying, certainly makes life much easier. I spent years running up and down my garden humping about cardboard boxes brimming with leaves, weeds and rubbish. *They* sagged, and so did I. Now I use a barrow. And, of course, it is enormously popular with children. Right-way up, or upside-down, in, on or under, there seems no end to its possibilities as a piece of creative play equipment, so it gives double value for money.

The only problem with barrows is that they are bulky things to store during the winter or soggy weather. There are some that will take apart so

that you can heave them up into the attic, or squeeze them into a corner of the garage or outhouse. Others can be left out of doors inside a large, heavy-weight, plastic bag, provided that you give it some ventilation holes. But your best plan is to try to find one made of totally weatherproof materials so that it can live outside quite happily the whole year round, saving time and trouble, and adding to its usefulness.

Practical Clothing
Whether or not you wear special clothes for gardening is very much a matter of personal preference, but two things are worth considering: pockets are useful – for string, labels, seed packets and so on – and protection is vital.

Sturdy shoes not only keep your feet dry and make digging more comfortable, they also prevent you from chop-

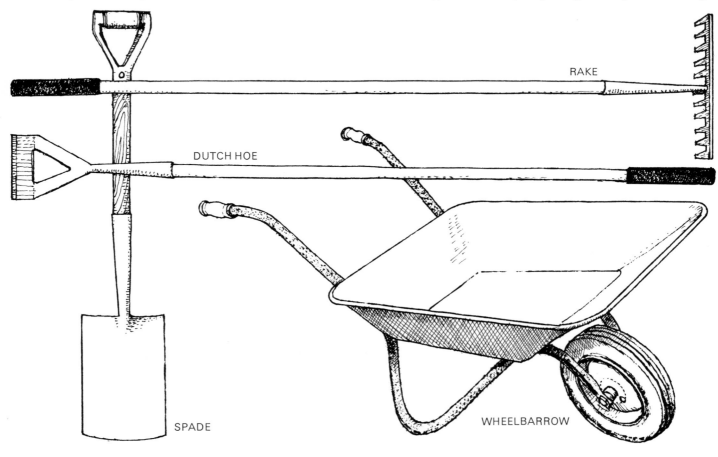

RAKE

DUTCH HOE

SPADE

WHEELBARROW

ping off your toes if your aim with the spade is erratic.

Some delicate jobs must be done with bare hands but if, for instance, you're hacking back the undergrowth, sorting out the nettles, or pruning prickly stems, you'll suffer less if you wear gloves.

I often prefer to kneel down when I'm gardening, but I do hate getting the knees of my jeans wet and muddy. There are gardening kneelers on the market, of course, but they are just one more thing to cart around and they tend to get left behind in the shrubbery when you've rushed off to the rose beds. There are also tie-on, waterproof knee-pads, but these, I think, are expensive gimmicks for the gift trade rather than gardening necessities. I've solved the problem to my own satisfaction by simply fastening a flat plastic bag over each knee with a couple of safety pins. It costs me nothing, it's practicable, and best of all, I don't have to wash my trousers, or my knees, every time I want to do a spot of gardening.

Above: A plastic wheelbarrow doubles as a garden toy for an active child.

Left: Tools should last a lifetime if chosen with care. Many styles and different materials are available, so before buying check up on the weight, blade size if applicable, type of handle and length of shaft — unless comfortable and well balanced gardening will become a tiring chore. Stainless steel is best but expensive. With all tools take the time to clean them properly and wipe them over with an oily rag after use.

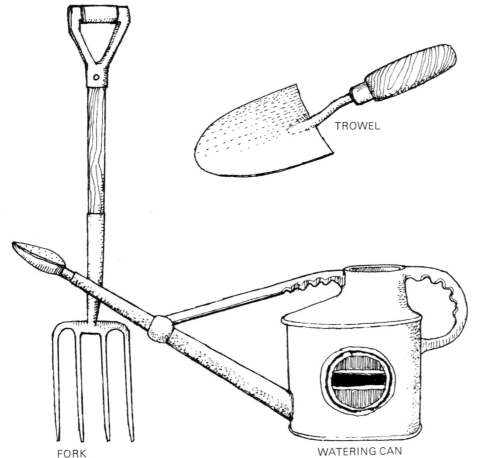

TROWEL

FORK

WATERING CAN

Getting to Know Your Garden

Whether you are tackling a brand-new garden, or one overdue for renovation, don't lay even a finger on it before you've planned your layout. Work out very carefully who and what your garden is for, and give more consideration to meeting the needs of your own family rather than impressing the neighbours with the greenness of your fingers and the impeccability of your taste.

To start with, you should give realistic and practical deliberation to the climate in your part of the country and the position of your garden, and then to the type and condition of your soil.

If you can count on long, warm, dry summers, and your garden is a sheltered suntrap, plan for outdoor living, invest in garden furniture and a large and handsome sunshade, and make it easy to eat, and even work, alfresco.

Lightweight, plastic-coated furniture is by far the most practicable since, unlike wood or iron, it can get soaked or scorched without deteriorating. It's sensible to buy very pretty chairs and tables so that they can do double-duty indoors and solve any problems that arise when the house is full of friends and visitors.

It's also a good idea to have a long lead, plus plug and socket, so that you

Make a moveable screen and take your 'privacy' around the garden with you.

can take electrical equipment on to your terrace with you and work in the sunshine. I have a secluded, quiet garden, so I always type outside when the weather is good enough, as well as using iron, sewing machine and electric drill on the patio. I have a telephone extension out there too.

You could add to your privacy and protection by making a movable screen which is also a frame for tall or climbing plants. All you need is a long, strong trough, mounted on sturdy castors, and supporting a frame of trellising backed, if you wish, by rigid plastic sheeting. Fill the container with compost, plant it with a sweet-scented honeysuckle or climbing rose, see that it is well drained, fed and watered, and it will give you a dense, green, fragrant wall to place where you please. Alternatively you could fill the trough with pot plants of your choice and take them indoors in harsh weather.

If you suffer from long, cold winters and damp summers, and if your garden provides little shelter from the elements, *don't* fight, capitulate. Budget for a conservatory extension to your house, a warm, green haven where you – and your more delicate plants – can flourish in comfort and style.

Every Garden has Its Problems

Gardens are like husbands – no two are alike.

Each one has its own special needs and desires. Each one will bloom and flourish given loving care and individual attention, but neglect its personal requirements, ride roughshod over its cries for help, and it will grow nasty.

Of course, you may be fortunate enough to have a well-tempered, equable plot with a sunny disposition and no personality problems at all. If so, your life together will be roses all the way!

But if it *has* got a few disaster areas, you're going to have to come to terms with them. It's just no good thinking you'll be able to reform it once the honeymoon is over – it will stubbornly resist all attempts at reclamation. Better to accept it the way it is, warts and all.

I write from experience, back-breaking, hand-blistering experience. In my first year as a gardener I made every mistake in the book. I was the fool who tried to grow vegetables in full shade. I was the idiot who insisted that I *could* grow rhododendrons on limy soil. I was the one who was determined to transform my heavy, waterlogged clay into light, friable loam even if it killed me. And it nearly did.

But at last I learnt the simple lesson that was staring me in the face. Every soil, every situation, has its own natural vegetation. All you have to do is to find out which plant families like to grow there, and then plant it up with the most beautiful species you can find.

Encourage its idiosyncrasies, don't try to thwart them. Discover where the sun never shines, where the soil is like a quagmire, and plant it accordingly. But first – know your soil.

Finding Out about the Soil

The most sensible, efficient and modern method of testing the acidity or alkalinity of your soil is to buy and use a soil-testing kit. There are many on the market, reasonably priced, easy to use and provided with full instructions. If you are of a scientific turn of mind, and yearn nostalgically for

A soil-testing kit.

happy days spent in the school lab., this is the method for you. You'll thoroughly enjoy tinkering with test-tubes and litmus paper.

A more companionable method is to chat up your neighbours about what grows – or refuses to grow – in their gardens. This is really very effective. It also helps you to make new friends and often leads to a mutually beneficial plant- and equipment-swopping scheme. I can recommend it.

The third and final method is to learn to read your weeds. Whenever they appear, they tell a story. For instance, a sudden crop of daisies can indicate an acid soil, lacking in lime, as can sorrel, plantain and mayweed. Campanula, scarlet pimpernel and bladder campion flourish on chalky soil. If the soil is heavy it will attract coltsfoot, dandelion and creeping buttercup. If it is light and sandy it will prove a natural habitat for shepherd's purse, cornflower and spurrey. If you have a rampant crop of horsetails, the chances are the soil will be damp, clayey and badly drained. If groundsel flowers repeatedly in one season when it is only about 5 cm (2 in) high the soil is lacking in fertility, and if clovers and vetches grow happily it is probably deficient in nitrogen.

The other clever thing about weeds is that they tend to cure, or at least improve, the deficiencies of the soil they grow in, so you needn't feel honour-bound to eradicate them ruthlessly. In fact, the wise gardener leaves

DAISY

SORREL

PLANTAIN

MAYWEED

CAMPANULA

SCARLET PIMPERNEL

BLADDER CAMPION

COLTSFOOT

DANDELION

his weeds alone unless they are actually attacking young plants and seedlings, or creating an eyesore, because, as a rule, they tend to do much less harm than good.

Daisies, as they die and decompose, will enrich the soil with calcium, cancelling out its lime deficiency.

Sorrel's long taproot will bring up nutrients from the subsoil.

Coltsfoot, thistles and dandelions have penetrating roots which will help to aerate heavy clay.

Clovers and vetches have root nodules which store nitrogen, so if you cut off their tops and leave the roots to decay in the ground, the soil will benefit.

However, the uncrowned king of all the weeds is the stinging nettle, whose benefits are legion. It is a plant which has the ability to stimulate the growth of all other plants growing nearby, and to make them more resistant to disease. It can improve the yield and quality of soft fruits, and it can improve the essential oils in aromatic herbs. It is also the caterpillar food of the Peacock and Tortoiseshell butterflies, so if you value these beautiful insects you should leave a patch of nettles for them.

When you have done your soil checks and decided whether it is acid or alkaline, heavy or light, wet or dry, shady or sunny, you will find it quite easy to choose the right plants for it. The two most extreme soil types you are likely to encounter are clay and chalk.

CREEPING BUTTERCUP   SHEPHERD'S PURSE   CORNFLOWER

SPURREY   BINDWEED   GROUNDSEL   CLOVER

VETCH   THISTLE   STINGING NETTLE

Coping with Clay

If you are gardening on clay you will know about it in every bone of your body. In dry weather it will be as hard as rock and riddled with cracks. In wet weather it will be heavy, sticky, water-logged and impossible.

One or two simple do's and don'ts will help to improve it.

Do make a habit of adding to it any ashes you may have from an open fire. They will help to lighten it. Leaves and peat are a useful addition too.

Don't be too keen to banish long-rooted weeds growing there. They are helping to aerate the soil for you.

Do dig over any unplanted earth quite roughly at the beginning of winter. The frosts will help to break it up.

Don't walk on it when it's damp. You will make it compacted and even heavier. If you really need to move about on it in wet weather a few strategically placed stepping stones, made from broken paving or two bricks set together on their sides, will make access easy.

The good news about clay is that it is normally acid, or low in lime, and very fertile, and that lots of lovely,

When digging is required it is easier in the long run to do it properly. First, remove a trench (the width and depth of the spade blade) of soil and place this in a pile at the end of the plot. Then turn each spadeful of soil forward, keeping the trench open as you go. Incorporate well-rotted compost or manure into the trench as you work. Finally fill in the last trench with the heap of soil removed at the beginning.

easy-care shrubs particularly enjoy growing in it. The most famous are the azaleas and rhododendrons, which live in natural neighbourliness with the mainly lime-hating heathers. The flowering currant, ribes, will flourish here, the fascinating pernettya with its berries of pink and white, and some types of magnolia, as well as cornus, deutzia and diervilla.

Most herbaceous plants will do well enough too, provided that they are planted in the spring in soil that has been well broken up. Primulas especially will thrive in heavy, clayey land as long as it does not dry out just after they have flowered, so it's a good idea to grow them under partial shade.

If Chalk is the Problem
With chalky soil you have more or less the same problems, only in reverse. Instead of being heavy and wet it is so light that it can't hold water and dries out almost immediately. You can help matters a little by spreading compost on top of the ground, around the plants, during the spring, and then digging in what is left during the autumn.

Lime-lovers which will flourish here are legion. Clematis, for instance, is a native plant of the chalklands, as are campanulas, dianthus and scabious. Among the shrubs, brooms are naturals, as well as wisteria and buddleia, the butterfly bush.

Many of the prettiest garden plants are chalk lovers.

Among the perennials, choose especially Michaelmas daisies, chrysanthemums and the handsome penstemons.

In fact, most flowers, shrubs, fruit and vegetables are tolerant of a certain amount of lime, but it is death to the rhododendron family. If you have a lot of lime and a love of this particular family don't languish sadly without them. Cheat nature, and plant them in tubs, or in raised beds made from peat blocks and filled with a peaty soil mixture. But do remember to water them with rainwater – the chances are that there's lime in the water that comes out of your taps.

Turning Shade to Advantage

Nearly every garden has a shady corner or border which needs special planting.

Few plants will thrive under densely planted trees – they can't get enough light, food or water after the trees have taken their share. My own solution when faced with this problem was to pave beneath the trees, and to enliven the paving with pots of shade-loving plants which I moved about from time to time so that they didn't live their entire lives in green gloom.

Much easier is the dappled shade cast by more open tree-planting. A wild, woodland garden can be a joy to the eye – and to the nose. Here you can plant bulbs like snowdrops and scillas, alliums, anemones and aconites, dog's-tooth violet (*Erythronium dens-canis*) and the mysterious snake's-head fritillary (*Fritillaria meleagris*). Here primulas and primroses will thrive, periwinkle (vinca) and London pride (*Saxifraga umbrosa*) provide ground cover, rhododendrons give greenery throughout the year, and honeysuckle and *Clematis montana* scramble happily up trees and fencing to give height and colour as well as fragrance.

Finally, add a few plants of sweet white woodruff, *Asperula odorata*. The flowers and leaves, when pressed, smell of new mown hay and were at one time used for scenting linen, a custom you might like to revive.

Below left and right: If you have a chalky soil and want to grow acid-loving plants, such as azaleas, then consider making a special peat bed. Use blocks of peat as bricks to make the retaining walls and fill in with an acid compost.

Opposite top right: It may be best to pave in heavily shaded areas rather than attempt to grow plants here. Do not take the paving slabs right up to the tree trunk as they are likely to get lifted by the larger roots. Instead fill in between with gravel.

Opposite bottom right: These elegant containers of hostas make a splendid feature for a shady corner of the garden.

Once a garden like this is established it is self-perpetuating and will need little more than occasional thinning out to keep it beautiful.

Whenever possible, incorporate white or pastel-coloured flowers when you're planting beneath trees. They reflect the light and glimmer with pale beauty in the shade, shining out, especially at dusk, from the encircling darkness (see page 116).

If your shade is cast by tall buildings or walls you might prefer a more formal garden. If so, I would recommend you to think green and become acquainted with the handsome hosta family, valued chiefly for its foliage. *Hosta sieboldiana* has superb blue-green leaves and early summer flowers of pale lilac, *H. plantaginea* flowers later, with huge sweet-scented white trumpets. Other hosta species well worth considering are *crispula*, *undulata* and *fortunei albopicta*. If you find the names rather fearsome ask for it by its popular name of plantain lily, and see what your nurseryman comes up with.

Useful shade-tolerant flowers which combine gracefully with hostas are the beautiful ground-cover plants, epimedium and dicentra, the fragrant *Primula auricula*, and *Lilium regale* with its pervading summer perfume. This one likes its roots in shade, but some sunshine for its beautiful head.

Where there is room for shrubs don't neglect *Daphne mezereum*, the japonica camellias and winter-flowering *Viburnum fragrans*, and finally, clothe that wall with the winter jasmine, *Jasminum nudiflorum*, and forsythia so that it will glow with gold from dead of winter to late spring.

Where it's Wet

If there is a damp area in your garden you don't need to involve yourself in the agonies of draining it. Transform it, instead, into a beautiful bog!

There are many lovely plants which will thrive in wet – but not waterlogged – conditions, especially in dappled light. Among the easier are members of the primula family, especially the candelabra types with whorls of flowers up the stems, and the later flowering *florindae*, or Himalayan cowslip. Primulas live very happily alongside the superb blue *Meconopsis betonicifolia*, the Himalayan poppy, so plant them

together as loving neighbours. This is also the spot for the early spring kingcup, *Caltha palustris*, and the dainty water forget-me-not, *Myosotis palustris*. (By the way, *palustris* means 'marsh' so you can hardly go wrong with a plant with this surname.) For instance, another good plant for this situation is *Euphorbia palustris*, the flower arranger's delight, with its unusual greenish-yellow flowers. Some irises love water too, especially the hybrids of *Iris sibirica*, and the spectacular *Iris kaempferi* which has huge, decorative flowers in an entrancing variety of shades from white to royal purple.

Later in the summer astilbes will thrive here, as well as hemerocallis (the day lily), mimulus and bergamot. Finally, in a shaded corner, ferns of all kinds will flourish, ranging from the low-growing hart's-tongue, phyllitis, to osmunda, the majestic royal fern.

If you would like to have a bog garden, but there is not a suitable wet patch, don't despair. You can make one very easily. Simply excavate an area of soil not less than 1-m (approximately 3-ft) square to a depth of 45 cm (18 in), and line the hole with plastic sheeting. Make a few small holes at

Below: Cross section through a bog garden
Opposite: Plants in many shades of green make a restful corner in this cool, shady garden. The bold leaf shapes are especially important in giving form and texture to such a grouping.

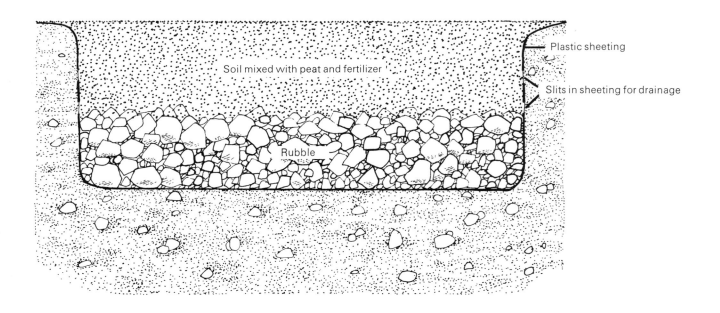

Plastic sheeting

Slits in sheeting for drainage

Soil mixed with peat and fertilizer

Rubble

30-cm (12-in) intervals about 15 cm (6 in) up from the base. Place inside a 15-cm (6-in) layer of rubble. Return the excavated soil mixed with moist peat and a little general fertiliser, and you are ready to start planting.

Better still, if you have an old plastic paddling pool that has been punctured, puncture it a bit more and use it, un-inflated, instead of plastic sheeting.

Needless to say, you will have to keep your bog garden very thoroughly watered during dry weather.

When it's Hot and Dry
If you have a hot, dry garden, go for the sun-lovers which can survive a certain amount of drought. There are, in fact, a surprising number to choose from.

The splendid tobacco plants, nicotiana, and petunias flourish in heat, and though these are bedding plants they are worth taking a little trouble with because of the summer pleasure they give. The same can be said of the prostrate Livingstone daisy, mesembryanthemum, which looks fabulous massed in full sun. Don't, whatever you do, plant this one in partial shade. It will simply sulk and close its petals.

The most dramatic and glorious of the sun-worshipping perennials is the superb oriental poppy (*Papaver orientale*) with its huge, flamboyant flowers of orange scarlet, salmon pink and fiery red, but don't neglect the humbler double-flowered arabis and *Alyssum saxatile*, stonecrops (sedums) and houseleeks (sempervivums) because

they are sturdy growers, and trouble free. This is the spot for helianthemums too, for cranesbill (geranium) and potentilla, and the invaluable thyme family. Here saponaria will foam over a hot, dry bank in a froth of little rosy flowers, alongside the perennial iberis and dainty cistus.

Shrubs to plant include the invaluable broom family, *Senecio laxifolius*, escallonia, the little-known tree lupin, *Lupinus arboreus*, and the fragrant herbs, lavender and rosemary. And if you want a rose, go for varieties of the *Rosa spinosissima*, the burnet rose or scotch brier which should do well.

However, remember that all plants need water. Those I have suggested will do better than most in a dry spell, but all will enjoy a drink from time to time.

Remember also that you will need a certain amount of shade if you are to enjoy your garden to the full. If you have no trees or sheltering walls you would be wise to provide yourself with a movable umbrella or a mobile screen like the one described on page 14, or with canvas awnings or sunblinds fixed to your house or fencing. Any of these would make it a more comfortable and pleasant place.

With care and forethought your garden can be a beautiful extension to your living space, whatever its idiosyncrasies.

To save the chore of continual watering in hot, dry areas, grow some of the sun-loving plants like *Senecio laxifolius* (far left) or mesembryanthemum (left).
Above: Sunblinds can be both decorative and functional.

Plants for Clay

Bulbs:
Allium moly (golden garlic), Anemone, Camassia, Chionodoxa (glory of the snow), Colchicum (autumn crocus), *Fritillaria imperialis* (crown imperial), *Galanthus nivalis* (snowdrop), Hyacinth, Iris – some varieties, Leucojum (snowflake), Muscari (grape hyacinth), Narcissus (daffodil), Scilla (squill).

Perennials:
Althaea (hollyhock), *Anemone japonica* (Japanese anemone), Aster (Michaelmas daisy), Campanulas, Digitalis (foxglove), Geranium – some varieties, Helleborus (Christ-

Anemone japonica

mas rose), *Iris germanica*, Primula, Rudbeckia (Black-eyed Susan).

Shrubs:
Azalea, Berberis, Chaenomeles (japonica), Cornus, Deutzia, Diervilla, Erica (heather), Forsythia, Hypericum, Kalmia, Lonicera (honeysuckle), Magnolia, Pernettya, Philadelphus (mock orange), Potentilla, Rhododendron, Ribes (flowering currant), Rose, Spiraea.

Trees:
Acer, Chamaecyparis, Crataegus (hawthorn), Laburnum, Malus, *Pinus bungeana* (lace-bark pine), Prunus, Sorbus (rowan).

Plants for Chalk

Hibiscus syriacus

Bulbs:
Most bulbs, *Crocosmia masonorum*, Cyclamen, Dahlia, Galtonia, Gladiolus, Nerine, Tulip.

Perennials:
Aster, Campanula, Dianthus, Eremurus, Eryngium (sea holly), Geum, Gypsophila, Helianthemum (sun rose), Papaver (poppy), Penstemon, Playcodon (balloon flower), Rudbeckia (Black-eyed Susan), Sage, Scabious, Solidago (golden rod).

Shrubs:
Berberis, *Buddleia davidii* (butterfly bush), Ceanothus, Cistus, Clematis, *Cornus mas*, Cytisus (broom), Deutzia, Forsythia, Fuchsia, Hebe, Hibiscus, Hypericum, Lavender, Lonicera (honeysuckle), Philadelphus (mock orange), Rosemary, Roses – most, Syringa (lilac), Weigela, Wisteria.

Trees:
Carpinus betula (hornbeam), *Fraxinus excelsior*, Malus (apple), *Morus nigra* (mulberry), Prunus, Sorbus (rowan, mountain ash).

Plants for Shade

Bulbs:
Allium triquetrum, Anemone, Convallaria (lily of the valley), *Cyclamen neapolitanum*, Endymion (bluebell), *Erythronium dens-canis* (dog's-tooth violet), *Fritillaria meleagris* (snake's-head fritillary), *Galanthus nivalis* (snowdrop), *Lilium regale*, Muscari (grape hyacinth), Polygonatum (Solomon's seal).

Perennials:
Aconite, Alchemilla, *Asperula odorata* (white woodruff), Astilbe, Cortaderia (pampas grass), Dicentra, Epimedium, Ferns, Hostas, *Lysimachia nummularia* (Creeping Jenny), *Primula auricula*, Primrose, *Saxifraga umbrosa* (London pride), Vinca (periwinkle).

Shrubs:
Camellia japonica, *Clematis montana*, *Daphne mezereum*, *Hedera helix* 'Cristata' (wavy leaved ivy), *Jasminum nudiflorum* (winter jasmine), *Mahonia aquifolium*, *Pieris japonica*, Philadelphus (mock orange), *Rubus biflorus*, *Rubus odoratus*, *Rubus* Tridel, Sarcococca (sweet box), Symphoricarpos (snowball bush), *Viburnum fragrans*.

Trees:
Acer griseum, *Stewartia sinensis*.

Plants for Damp Conditions

Bulbs:
Fritillaria meleagris (snake's head fritillary), *Iris kaempferi*, *Iris sibirica*, *Narcissus cyclamineus*.

Perennials:
Astilbe, *Caltha palustris* (kingcup), Eriophorum (cotton grass), *Euphorbia palustris*, Ferns, Hemerocallis (day lily), Lysichitum, *Meconopsis betonicifolia* (Himalayan poppy), Mentha (mint), Mimulus (monkey-flower), Monarda (bergamot), Scirpus (bulrush), Tradescantia, Trollius.

Shrubs:
Amelanchier lamarckii, *Calycanthus floridus* (allspice), Clethra, *Cornus alba* (red-barked dogwood), *Hippophae rhamnoides* (sea buckthorn), *Myrica gale* (bog myrtle), *Photinia villosa*, Sambucus (elder), Sorbaria, *Spiraea sanssouciana*, *Spiraea trichocarpa*, Symphoricarpos (snowball bush), Vaccinium.

Trees:
Alnus mitchelliana (American green alder), *Betula pendula*, *Crataegus oxyacantha*, *Magnolia virginiana*, Populus (poplar), *Pyrus communis* (pear).

Meconopsis betonicifolia

Plants for Hot and Dry Conditions

Bulbs:
Amaryllis belladonna, *Anemone blanda*, *Eremurus robustus* (foxtail lily), *Iris danfordiae*, *Nerine bowdenii*, *Schizostylis coccinea* (kaffir lily), *Sternbergia lutea* (winter daffodil), *Zephyranthes candida* (zephyr lily).

Perennials:
Alyssum saxatile (gold dust), Arabis (rock cress), Cistus, Geranium (cranesbill), Grasses such as *Briza media* (quaking grass), Helianthemum (sun rose), Helichrysum (everlasting-flower), Iberis (candytuft), Lychnis (campion), Mesembryanthemum (dorotheanthus), Oenothera, Saponaria (soapwort), Sedum (stonecrop), Sempervivum (houseleek), *Stachys lanata* (lamb's ear).

Shrubs:
Artemisia arborescens, Cistus, Cytisus (broom), Escallonia, Hypericum, Lavender, *Lupinus arboreus* (tree lupin), Potentilla, *Rosa spinosissima* varieties, Rosemary, *Senecio laxifolius*, Thyme.

Trees:
Ailanthus altissima (tree of heaven), *Ilex aquifolium*, *Robinia pseudoacacia* 'Frisia'.

Schizostylis coccinea

Oenothera glaber

Planning for Pleasure

When planning your garden it is important to think for the future, and remember that the needs of a family change constantly. If you hope to put down your roots for a good long stay you'll need to incorporate a 'flexibility factor' into your planning. Shakespeare saw seven ages in the life of man, but I only see four in the life of the average family.

Plan 1
The Starter Garden

Plan 2
The Nursery Garden

Plan 3
The Growing-up Garden

Plan 4
The Growing-old Garden

Plan 1
(see page 28)

The Starter Garden

Below: Imaginative use of paving and wood creates an outdoor extension to the living area.

To start with there is the young couple, new householders, quite probably both at work. The chances are they will have little time for gardening, but will want to enjoy what summertime leisure they have in the open air, re-laxing and entertaining their friends. They will also want their garden to provide them with flowers and per-haps a little food — fresh salads, for instance, a few herbs, and one or two choice vegetables.

Their ideal garden will feature a large, paved patio or terrace, in a sunny sheltered spot, preferably raised and near the house, and amply big enough to accommodate chairs, table, a port-

able barbecue and some tubs of flowers. It could be partially roofed, like a loggia, or given a striped canopy if extra shade or protection is required. An outside light will extend its usefulness, making it an ideal spot for late summer evenings, and a few well-placed garden torches will add party glamour for a special occasion.

A small herb garden can be situated near the back door, easily accessible even in the worst weather, and a small kitchen garden screened from view by a decorative hedge, and led up to and surrounded by a wide, hard, well-drained path. Who wants to wade through muddy puddles just to collect a lettuce?

Having established these essentials, the next problem is to decide exactly what to do with the space that hasn't been used up.

Right: The patio is an ideal place for a quiet cup of tea after a busy day.
Below: Equip your patio with a power point for lighting and add a barbeque for parties.

Furniture, Barbecues and Lighting

Get extra enjoyment out of your garden by introducing some fixtures and fittings. Here is a selection of furniture, lighting and barbeque equipment.

Opposite: Making a lawn.
Whether using seed or turf, the initial stages of lawn preparation are identical. After digging and weeding the ground, rake thoroughly to remove any large rubble which would otherwise work its way up through the grass. A level site is easier to cope with than a sloping one and it may be necessary to check with a plank and spirit level. Tread the soil to make it firm and rake again. To sow lawn seed evenly divide the area into yard-square sections and then scatter the seed at the rate of 55 g (2 oz) to each section. After sowing, rake over to get the seed just below the surface.

The turves are unrolled and laid so the joins are staggered and are then beaten flat so they are in contact with the earth below to encourage rooting. A topdressing of sand and peat is brushed into the crevices. The best times for sowing are early autumn or spring; turfing may be done at any time but avoid hot, dry spells.

Below: Use aluminium strip lawn edging to avoid a lot of laborious work.

Grass is Important

Although most gardening writers warn anyone wishing to avoid hard work to avoid grass like the plague, I disagree with them. I once tried living without a lawn and found it a most unhappy experience. I put down an area of paving stones, and planted herbs in all the cracks and chinks – only to find myself overwhelmed with difficult weeding. I pulled up the greenery and filled the gaps with cement – and then languished miserably in the concrete wilderness I had created. I hacked up some of the slabs and planted squares of chamomile – it lived sadly, and died within two years. And all the time I yearned for the colour of grass, the smell of grass and the feel of grass beneath my feet. I even yearned for the daisies that used to arrive as unbidden but welcome guests.

Perhaps I'm just a nature freak, but for me no garden is complete without a lawn. Besides, for the flexible garden that is going to grow with the family, it's a much better bet. When there are children playing it will be much more comfortable to fall down upon, and when alterations are called for – more space for growing vegetables, perhaps, or an extra flower bed – it's much easier to dig up and, eventually, to replace.

So, I would plant hard-wearing grass, using turves if quick results are more important than economy, but I would also invest in a good powered mower. I would cut the grass often, without using the hood, so that the clippings can be left where they fall. If the edges of the lawn are surrounded by narrow margins of brick, or aluminium lawn edging set just below the level of the grass, the mower can be run over them quite safely, the chore of edge-trimming avoided and hours of work saved.

It isn't necessary to have a wide, flowering border around the entire lawn, but it is pretty to have an occasional flowery peninsula erupting into it. If care is taken to concentrate only on spring-flowering bulbs, easy-care perennials and flowering shrubs, and to underplant them with sturdy ground-cover plants, maintenance can be kept to a minimum while the visual rewards are immense. Two or three rampant climbers will soften the rawness of new or bald fencing and have the added advantage of virtually looking after themselves and require only an occasional clipping.

Finally, for a finishing touch, and to give focus and shape, it would be pleasant to plant a tree in the lawn. My own choice, for a family garden, would be an apple tree, beautiful in blossom and delicious in fruit. With luck it will grow strong and sturdy along with the family, and eventually support a swing or hammock as well as give shade for a summer snooze, or afternoon tea with cucumber sandwiches!

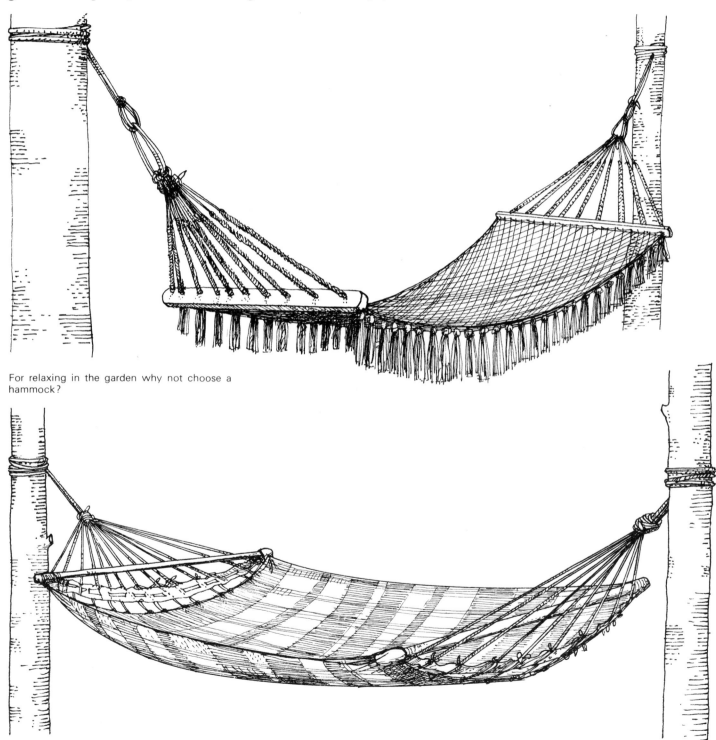

For relaxing in the garden why not choose a hammock?

Starter Garden Herb and Vegetable Collection

Herbs:
Chives, Mint, Parsley, Rosemary, Sage, Thyme.

Vegetables:
French beans, Ridge cucumber, Lettuce, Mangetout peas and/or asparagus peas, New potatoes, Rhubarb.

Easy-care, Grow-anywhere Plants

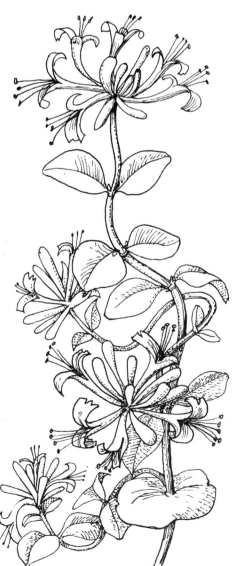

Bulbs:
Varieties of *Anemone blanda*, Crocus, *Galanthus nivalis* (snowdrop), Muscari, Narcissus.

Perennials:
Chosen varieties of Aster, Campanula, Centranthus (valerian), Doronicum, Geum, Iberis (candytuft), Pulmonaria, *Sedum spectabile*, Solidago (golden rod), Trollius.

Shrubs:
Chosen varieties of Berberis, Hebe, Hypericum, Lavender, Philadelphus and Spiraea. Also *Mahonia aquifolium* and *Senecio laxifolius*.

Ground Cover:
Chosen varieties of *Ajuga reptans*, Artemisia, Dianthus (pinks), Helianthemum, Lamium, *Lysimachia nummularia* (Creeping Jenny), *Mentha pulegium* (pennyroyal), *Stachys lanata*, Thyme and Vinca (periwinkle).

Hedging:
Chosen varieties of Copper beech, Rose.

Fence Flowers:
Chosen varieties of Rose and Lonicera (honeysuckle). Also *Clematis montana*, *Clematis tangutica*, *Jasminum nudiflorum* and *Polygonum baldschuanicum* (Russian vine).

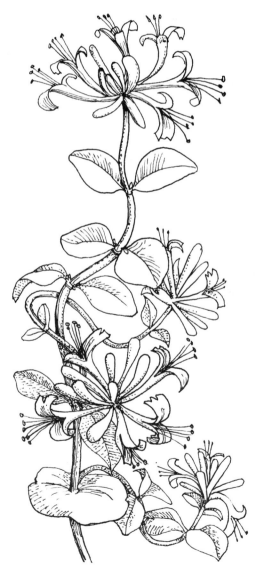

Plan 2

(see page 28)

The Nursery Garden

After a year or two, when there are young children in the family, the way the garden is used will probably change radically and it will begin to function largely as an outdoor nursery and playroom.

A family garden should, I think, be a place for children. A place where children can play, and rest, eat in the fresh air, watch birds and butterflies, spend time with their friends, and, eventually, begin gardening on their own accord.

So it goes without saying that children in the garden should not be screamed at to keep off the grass, mind the plants, and watch that ball. I don't believe that many youngsters are vandals by nature. If you explain to them quite simply that most of the things they see growing have been put there for a purpose, either to feed them, to attract wild life, or to make life more beautiful, they'll accept it and treat them with reasonable care. But that doesn't mean that accidents won't happen. Even if you plant hedges, or use nets and screens to protect flowering borders and the vegetable plot there's bound to be some damage.

Try not to let it worry you. The best solution is to plan for it. There's an old rhyme about sowing seeds that goes:

'One for the rook, one for the crow,
One to die, and one to grow',

and there's a lot of sense in that. Where there are children at play always try to plant more than you need so that, if one or two get destroyed, it's no great loss. Think about what you're planting too and avoid the rare or precious. Time enough for those when the children are grown.

Below: Small children love to play with water, but it is wiser to choose a collapsible plastic pool that can be packed away in the colder weather.

Making a Sandpit

Babies and tiny children need always to be within sight and sound of the adults who are looking after them, so the well-equipped patio will make an ideal place to park a pram and play-pen. It will also be the first playground, before the toddler becomes more mobile. Consequently, it makes a perfect site for a sandpit.

It is a good idea to lift and remove some of the slabs, excavate to a depth of about 45 cm (18 in), give the hole a lining of concrete, then, when absolutely dry and hard, fill it with sand. If the work is done carefully and the pit made quite watertight it can take on a new lease of life in years to come as a garden pool. In fact, you can save time and labour, though not money, if you take this idea one step further by forgetting about the concrete and simply investing in a very tough, flat-bottomed fibreglass pond and sinking this into the patio. Make sure that it is very firmly supported all around by earth and that the top edges are absolutely level, or it will never look quite right. Now you can fill it with sand while the children are little and change over to water when they are older and safer.

Sandpits can be of many kinds, **left**: a permanent structure of concrete and paving slabs, **below**: a sand-filled fibre glass pool. Both will later do duty as garden ponds. If there are no drainage holes, it is most important to ensure that the pit is covered after use with a piece of heavy-duty plastic sheeting. This will also stop any cats fouling the sandpits.

I wouldn't advise a permanent garden pool when there are toddlers around because water can be dangerous, even lethal. Babies love water, of course, but play safe and buy an inflatable paddling pool which can be emptied and put away when there is no adult in the garden.

Sand is safe, but it has a major problem. It attracts every cat for miles around and becomes a famous feline convenience. So do make a cover for the pit, and do make it strong and sturdy enough to walk on. That way you'll lose less of your guests next time you give a patio party. If the sandpit is in a less-frequented part of the garden, small mesh netting stretched on a wooden frame will make a sufficiently good cover.

Garden Toys
Other invaluable garden toys for little children are a safe swing, with an enclosed seat (set the paving stones you have removed from the patio for the sandpit into the lawn behind the swing where the 'pusher' will stand, and you will save a lot of wear and tear); a Wendy house, which will take to bits and fold flat for storage; a small climbing frame and a take-apart roundabout.

All of these can be bought from large toy shops but they are expensive. Much better, and more fun for the children, is to make some of these toys yourself.

The swing will probably be the only toy to need a permanent site in the garden, so place it carefully in a sunny, sheltered position. The others can be

moved around from time to time so that the grass doesn't get too worn in any one place. Try to ensure plenty of space around them to avoid bumps and pushes, and keep them well away from the flower borders if you value your blooms.

You will also have to get used to constant traffic movement in the form of tricycles, pedal cars, toy fire-engines, tractors, and so on, so banish your flowering tubs, and keep the patio and paths as clear of clutter as possible. If you find tracks are being worn away in the lawn, set in circuits of level, sunken stepping-stones and try to persuade the road-hogs to stick to them. You can always lift the stones and fill the gaps with turves at a later date if you wish, and in the meantime

you'll avoid the eyesore of a variegated and balding lawn.

Making a Home for a Pet
At this stage you might consider letting the children have a garden pet.

If a hedgehog happens to find you, make him a welcome visitor since he does no harm, and a whole lot of good, devouring pests like slugs, millipedes and caterpillars with devastating relish, while allowing the helpful ladybirds to live in peace. A regular supply of water and milk will encourage him to stay for a while, and a nesting box of his own could make him a permanent guest.

If you choose rabbits, give them a hutch facing south, and provide them with a little enclosed run where they can spend the daylight hours.

Below: There is a wide selection of children's garden toys to choose from; a number of these can easily be made by a handy parent.

Another popular pet is the guinea pig or cavy, but he needs to live in the garage or an outhouse during severe weather, so bear this in mind when you are making your choice.

You can make a simple cage from a sturdy wooden box, turned on its side, with the opening covered by a small panel of wood for privacy, and a larger, removable panel of chicken wire fastened to a light wooden frame. Other types of hutches can be bought from pet shops.

The best place to house an animal is in the working area of the garden – near the vegetable patch for easy feeding and cleaning.

Garden Utilities

This could also be the place for a garden shed if you need covered storage for all the paraphernalia of a growing family – tools, equipment, toys and foodstuffs, either for pets or bulk-bought for the family. If it's not pretty cover the shed with a rampant climber – the 'mile-a-minute' Russian vine, *Polygonum baldschuanicum*, for instance, which can grow 4·5 m (15 ft) in a season, and is smothered, during the summer months, with large, feathery bunches of creamy flowers.

Another thought. A young family engenders a lot of washing. If you hope to dry nappies and baby clothes outside, fix a space-saving rotary washing-line towards the bottom of the garden, with a hard path leading up to it, and

try to persuade the children to keep away from it. Sticky fingers on fresh laundry are *not* conducive to parental love. Your drying green will also form a buffer state between the children's playground and your vegetable garden and will consequently ensure a richer – and less-battered – crop.

When sharing a garden with young children you will discover that a certain amount of separation works wonders for family togetherness! And your tolerance will pay dividends in the long run because the chances are that if a child feels happy and at home in the garden, sooner or later he will turn into a gardener.

A Children's Garden
Children come to gardening by many various and devious routes. My own passion began as a result of a brainwave on the part of my father, who always did have rather eccentric ideas about child-rearing. For my seventh birthday he gave me a thoroughly original present – a sunny plot of land, half a dozen packets of fool-proof, quick-growing annual seeds, a few child-sized tools – and a load of steaming, stinking, absolutely splendid horse manure. I was enchanted. I toiled in my new garden all day and when the time came round for my birthday party it was only after floods of tears, a long

Opposite top: Encourage a friendly hedgehog to visit your garden, by putting down a saucer of milk.
Opposite bottom: If your clothes line is some distance from the house, lay a path or stepping stones so you can hang out the washing and remain dry shod.
Below: There are many ways of capturing a child's imagination in garden games. A 'flower show' can provide such entertainment as the children select and arrange a small posy of flowers. However, it may be necessary to give 'firsts' all round to keep the peace!

hot bath and a thorough deodorising, that I could be buttoned into my party dress and led out to greet my guests.

I've quite forgotten what my party was like, but I remember to this day the results of my first attempts at gardening. Given a completely free hand I had done a magnificent job of dung-spreading, then scattered my seeds in glorious abundance, in artistic swirls and patches. Nothing so dull as straight lines for me. A few weeks later I had marigolds the size of cauliflowers, cornflowers more like chrysanthemums and Californian poppies that seemed convinced that they hailed from the Himalayas. For sheer, dense, dazzling colour I've never since achieved anything quite as good, despite my adult experience. From that time on, as far as gardening was concerned, I was hooked for life.

My own children's indoctrination was rather different. They're both strong-minded individuals, and any tentative suggestion that they might like to help in the garden invariably met with a polite, but firm, negative. But what I couldn't achieve was effected in the end by a mouse, their pet mouse, Snow White. You may not see any obvious connection between mice and gardening, but it's actually quite simple. Even in the best-regulated of households mice have a habit of dying after a year or so, and then they have to be buried – in the garden. Snow White's minute corpse had to be consigned to the earth with full ceremonial honours, and then her tiny grave had to be beautified and tended with loving care. In the centre they erected a little cross inscribed with the touching epitaph,

'A HOUSE WITH A MOUSE
IS A HAPPY HOUSE',

CORNFLOWER

NEMESIA

ALYSSUM

CANDYTUFT

NEMOPHILA

44

and around it they planted little clumps of primula, violets and pansies. Enriched with good mousey humus, watered by their abundant tears, the plants flourished. And since it would have seemed somehow disrespectful of Snow White's immortal memory to neglect her garden of remembrance, the boys weeded it and added bits and pieces, and gradually without realising it, almost despite themselves, they turned into gardeners.

Six weeks later a puppy healed their broken hearts, and Snow White was forgotten, but not their garden. It got bigger and more beautiful day by day, and eventually became a showpiece.

There's a moral here somewhere. Perhaps that you can lead a child to gardening, but you can't make him.

It is important to remember that children work to a different time-scale from that of the adult world. It's no good holding out hopes of next year's crop – what they want are almost instant results. They need seeds or plants that will very rapidly give them some sign of success. Candytuft is useful, a quick-flowering annual which will grow easily almost anywhere, and cornflower and calendula, especially the Scotch marigold Radio, are also valuable. It's a good idea, I think, to persuade them to intersperse the rows or drifts of seeds with a few young plants which will absorb their interest and give them something to watch while they are waiting for germination to take place. One or two nasturtiums, some alyssum, nemesia and nemophila (baby blue eyes), can be bought for a small outlay. They will grow well and flower freely, providing colour enough to satisfy the children without making too great demands on their skill as fledgling gardeners. And if the flowers are admired and taken indoors to decorate the house their pride will be enormous.

Many children have an interest in the oddities of the world of horticulture as well as the beauties. A couple of annual sunflowers can be a daily source of wonder. In a sunny, open position, and on really fertile soil, *Helianthus annuus* can grow as tall as 3 m (10 ft), and the miniature gardener will find great pleasure, and profit, in measuring its daily growth. At the other end of the size scale, the tiny leptosiphon delights through its very smallness.

Nasturtium Sandwiches

Let children eat the flowers they have grown too – they'll find the idea quite fascinating. Nasturtium sandwiches are a good idea for a summer picnic. Make them from white and brown bread, mayonnaise, finely chopped cooked chicken, seasoning and a bunch of washed nasturtiums.

For six sandwiches, butter the bread generously. Mix a cupful of chicken with a quarter of a cupful of mayonnaise, salt and pepper, and ten chopped nasturtium leaves, and spread the brown bread with the mixture. Cover with a layer of nasturtium petals, letting some of them stick out in a frill around the edges, then add the top slices of white bread.

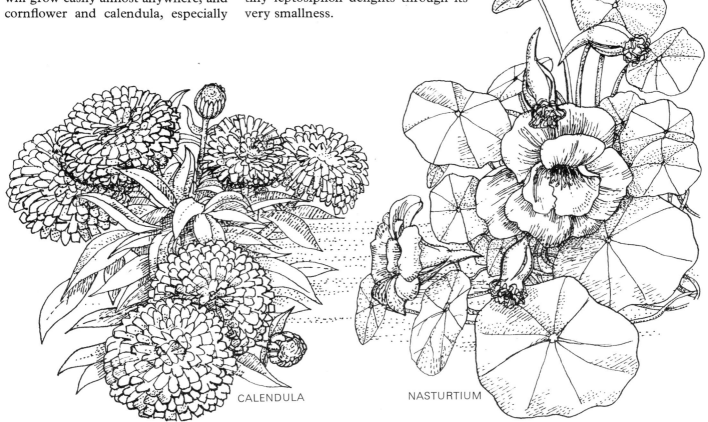

CALENDULA   NASTURTIUM

Games with Flowers

Some flowers can be used in children's games. Daisy chains, dandelion clocks, buttercups-under-the-chin, and 'He loves me, he loves me not', played with daisy petals, are all part of the ancient ritual of childhood. The old cottage garden favourite, antirrhinum, or snapdragon, is fun because of its little rabbit heads, and jaws that can indeed be made to snap. The silvery pods of honesty can be used as counters or pretend money or treasure. And pansies have hidden fascinations too.

Pick a pansy head and remove the petals carefully, leaving the five green sepals of the calyx. Snip off the two in front and you'll reveal a little man sitting in a chair, a red scarf about his neck, his feet in a tub. If you want to see his rather skinny little legs simply slit the tub with your finger-nail, peel it away, and there they are.

Choose a large poppy.

Pull its petals down and paint on a face.

Slip the stalk between the petals to make arms.

Finally, tie a blade of grass around the dolly's waist.

To make a dolly from a poppy, choose the largest bloom you can find, gently pull its petals down, inside out, so that they look like a skirt around the top of the stalk. Now you will see the dolly's head. Pull the hairs off one side to make a face, and draw on it eyes, nose and mouth. Cut off the bottom half of the stalk and slip it through the top of the petals to form arms, then fasten a blade of grass round the poppy dolly's waist to make her dress billow out gracefully.

Hollyhock ladies can entrance little children too. Turn an opened blossom upside down as the lady's body. Using a small sharp piece of twig, fix on a hollyhock bud at the top, to look like a head, and slip another little twig through the calyx, just below the head, to form the arms. Any bell-shaped flower can be set upon the hollyhock head as a bonnet, and a nasturtium

leaf skewered on to a straight twig will make a parasol for the lady. If you stand the finished figure on the surface of a bowl of water and blow at it gently it will float about enchantingly.

Even simpler is grandma-in-a-bonnet. Pick a nice big daisy, draw a happy smiling face on the yellow centre, trim round the petals to give them straight edges, but leave the two below the chin to hang down as bonnet ribbons, and you've made a jolly little old lady.

Pick a daisy.

Paint on a cheerful face.

Trim petals to form grandma-in-a-bonnet.

Vegetable Growing can be Fun

It's unlikely, however, that a young gardener will want to concentrate on flowers alone. He will probably have fun growing just one or two easy vegetables and salads too. I still remember the thrill of treasure trove when I unearthed my very first potatoes, some of them not much bigger than marbles, but how delicious they tasted, boiled in a pot and eaten on their own with lashings of melted butter. Honey-sweet peas too, pinched from the pod, still warm from the sun. None that I grow now can match that memory for flavour. Broad beans and dwarf French beans are often favourites with children, both for growing and eating, and one or two early-maturing turnips could be grown as an appetising accompaniment. Quite a young child should be able to cope with a little row of lettuce, and he could try his hand at growing radishes too, starting with Sparkler, which is very crisp and sweet and ready for the table three weeks after sowing.

Of course, it's very important that the fruits of his labours should always be used, admired and enjoyed. Once he has seen the family sitting down to a dish of his own vegetables, or eating crisp salads freshly cut from his own garden, it's almost certain that he'll be an addicted gardener for life.

But if he is to have this sort of success he must have a good piece of land, about 3 by 2 m (10 by 6 ft) to start with. Give him a sunny plot of light, well-drained soil – not, please not, a dark, dank corner which would try the patience of a professional – provide him with trouble-free seeds and plants, and then leave him to get on with it. The chances are, he will astonish you. A junior gardener doesn't think in the same way as an adult. He tends to have a lofty contempt of regimentation. He sees no reason why vegetables and flowers and salads should not be grown together in glorious abundance. He draws no artificial distinctions between cultivated flowers and their wild country cousins. He is liable to make a pebble road through his terrain and drive toy cars along it, or get out his building set and make a miniature village bang in the middle of it. But why not? His garden will have a charm and gaiety all its own.

So, curb your tongue, give advice only when it's asked for, show a real appreciation of his work – and you may even find that in a year or two he will be giving you a hand in *your* garden.

Children will enjoy the garden more if given a sunny spot where plants will flourish.

Plan 3

(see page 29)

The Growing-up Garden

As the family gets older, with children stretching into their teens, the garden will need to adapt again to fit its needs.

The patio will be the perfect place for teenage parties as well as adult entertaining, so it might well be worth discarding the portable barbecue and building in a permanent one. Get the youngsters to help and they'll treat it with extra care and respect.

Building a Barbecue
Basically, a barbecue is simply a grid of iron propped up over a space in which fuel can be burnt. However, if you enjoy eating food cooked in the open air it is worth taking the trouble to build something more elaborate, which will also provide a surface for food preparation, and storage for fuel.

Build a brick wall, table-high and about 1·5 m (4½ ft) long. Build three more walls at the same height, jutting out at right angles from the back wall, and equally spaced, so that you have two compartments. You can use one of these for cooking, the other for preparation and storage. The two walls enclosing the cooking section will need two sets of ledges, one near the top to support an iron grid for cooking, one about 30 cm (1 ft) below to support an iron sheet on which the fire will be laid.

Fix a slab of marble or solid wood from the central wall to the other outside wall and use this as your counter. Make a door for the space beneath and use it for keeping implements, bags of charcoal, and so on.

Since you've already provided for an electric socket outside the youngsters will be able to take their records into the garden for summer-time dancing and enjoyment.

By now the sandpit will have become something of an anachronism, so it can be emptied and turned into a fish pond or garden pool.

Right: Encourage teenagers to entertain their friends at home with hamburgers and sausages cooked on a home-made barbecue.
Opposite: Permanent barbecues can be easily constructed from bricks and will provide hours of fun as both family and guests do their own cooking. Charcoal is the most suitable fuel and it is important to make sure that it is very hot and glowing before any food is placed on the grill. Any meat or fish can be cooked in this way. Kebabs with the addition of fruits such as peaches or pineapple are extremely good.
Overleaf: From barbecue to table, the family enjoys lunch out of doors.

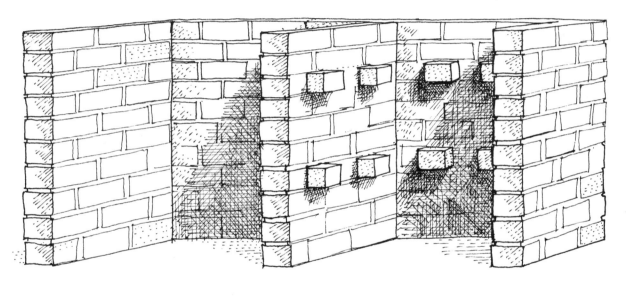

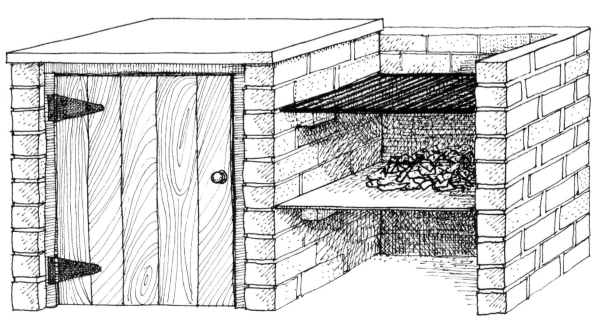

Making a Garden Pool

To turn your sandpit into a pool, first empty it, then clean it, fill it with water and leave it to stand for a few days. (Don't waste the sand – use it to lighten any patches of heavy soil you have in the vegetable garden. You'll find that it will help crops such as carrots to thrive.)

Consult a water garden specialist about the best species of plants for your particular climate and the situation of your pool. Choose a suitable water lily, plant it in a basket, cover the soil with washed shingle and submerge it just below the surface of the water, propping it up on bricks if necessary. Next, plant a couple of oxygenators like the water violet, hottonia, and the water starwort, *Callitriche verna*. Now you are ready to add two or three goldfish. They will survive the winters without difficulty provided that the water is not allowed to remain frozen. Do remember to *melt* the ice – if you break it too violently you can kill the fish.

Left: Planting a water lily.
Below: A small formal pool can be a most worthwhile feature in a courtyard garden, adding much to the design and bringing a new interest by way of water plants and fish.

Garden Games

A lot of the early garden toys will have lost their charm, and can now be replaced by their more grown-up counterparts. Those that kept all of my family happy, including grandparents, for many years, and which had the added advantage of not causing too much havoc among the plants, included: a bounce-back; garden 'tennis', with an anchored ball; football goal-posts, with a netting back and sides to restrain the ball; croquet and an old tyre, suspended by rope, which doubled as swing and target-mouth for throwing games.

Again, all of these except the last can be bought quite easily in toy stores and games shops, but it would probably be well worth making the goal-posts. Use 5-cm (2-in) square, treated timber for the posts, and garden netting anchored with guy ropes.

Ball games are bound to cause some damage to plants, but it's best to bow to the inevitable with as good a grace as you can muster. A nagging, complaining parent will only succeed in driving the children away eventually. Personally, I would choose a garden filled with happy youngsters rather than prize blooms any day. Time enough when they have left home to become garden-proud.

So console yourself with the fact that most of the plants in your borders are tough specimens specially chosen for their resilience (see page 37), and enjoy your young family while you have the chance.

Growing children inevitably mean growing foodbills. This may be the time when you will want to extend both vegetable and herb garden, and find room for a few fruit bushes – blackberries and raspberries are particularly good value as they crop well and are easily grown.

The keen family gardener might even like to sacrifice some of the lawn and enlarge the flower beds and borders to incorporate some of the special features suggested later in the book.

Very gradually, your garden, like your family, is growing and changing shape.

With some ingenuity, games for older children can be included in even a small garden. Suspend an old tyre from a strong tree branch or place a netball or basketball target ring at a suitable height. Croquet sets are expensive, but can sometimes be bought second hand and provide hours of fun as one's cunning in the game increases.

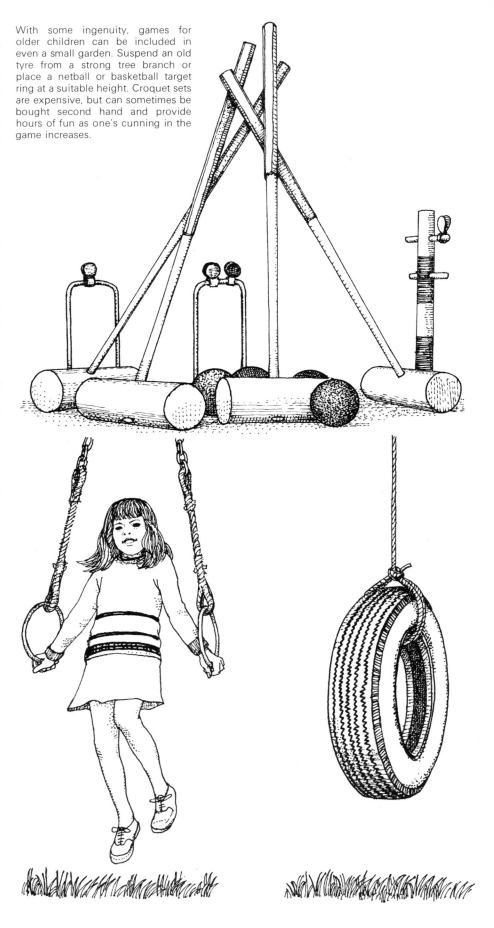

Plan 4

(see page 29)

The Growing-old Garden

It is one of life's sad ironies that when the young have grown up and left home their parents frequently find that they have more and more time for gardening, but less and less strength and energy.

Now is the time for them to look ahead, and to make sure that their garden is arranged in such a way that in years to come it will give a maximum of pleasure, combined with a minimum of effort.

Often the middle-aged have to care for an elderly, possibly handicapped, relative. If this is so, it's wise to think of their needs too. For instance, an old person, or one in a wheelchair, cannot bend down easily but might still like to grow flowers. Tubs, urns, pots, troughs and low-hanging or wall-mounted baskets are the best solution to this problem, especially if they are placed about the patio so that they are easily accessible. The planting up of containers and hanging baskets is described later in the book, see pages 74 to 76.

If the herb garden and borders now seem too large for comfortable care, they can be partially grassed over, or given a surround of paving stones which will cut down the working area and make an attractive visual feature. Remember to embed them in concrete to eliminate weed problems.

Alternatively some sections of the border can be made into raised beds. If peat blocks are used to contain the soil, the bed makes an ideal home for heathers, azaleas, rhododendrons, primulas and cyclamen. Another idea is a hollow brick wall or a trough garden which can be filled with soil to become an alpine garden. Gardens like these which can be tended without stooping or kneeling are an enormous boon to the elderly. They can also be reached from a wheelchair.

Making a Trough Garden

Sadly, there don't seem to be many genuine stone troughs going for a song any longer, but it's quite easy to make a

Gardening is one activity which need not be denied the elderly or handicapped if some thought is given to the arrangement of the garden. Raised beds 60 cm (2 ft) and 120 cm (4 ft) wide, made from bricks or concrete blocks, bring vegetables and flower gardening within the scope of someone in a wheelchair.

reasonably good imitation from an ordinary glazed sink.

First you need to give it an overcoat of 'hypertufa'; this is made from one part of cement, two and a half parts of sand and one and a half of peat, mixed together with just sufficient water to form a malleable consistency. Paint the sides of the sink with a bonding agent, and when this is tacky, cover it with a layer of hypertufa about 1 cm ($\frac{1}{2}$ in) thick, beginning at a bottom corner and working upwards. Eventually this will weather to look like natural stone.

Alpine and rock plants provide a specialised interest and a good hobby subject for both young and old alike. They have the advantage that they can be grown easily in troughs or raised beds. This small circular bed makes a delightful focal point for a conveniently placed garden seat.

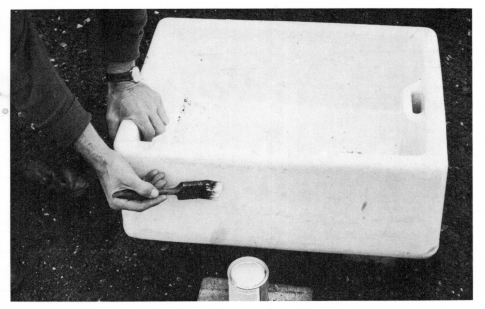

Fit a piece of perforated zinc, to keep out pests, over the drainage hole, and put some broken crocks on top. Now fill the bottom of the sink with a layer of chippings, cover them with a layer of peat, or turves turned upside down, and fill it up with suitable compost – nothing very rich or the plants will grow too luxuriantly.

Arrange a few pieces of rock in the top, burying them well into the compost so that they are firmly embedded, and interplant the crevices. Complete the planting with alpines of your choice, and finally cover the soil with a layer of stone chippings to prevent it from drying out, and to keep the roots cool.

The trough should be placed on brick pedestals about 45 cm (18 in) high – this will assist drainage and keep out the slugs, and the tiny plants will be easier to enjoy and tend.

The best situation for an alpine trough is a slightly shaded position facing either west or east.

Making a trough garden from an old sink
Top left: After cleaning the sink thoroughly, paint with a bonding agent.
Centre left: Cover with a layer of hypertufa working upwards from the base of the trough, and taking it over the edge and down the inside for about 10 cm (4 in). Finish off with a trowel.
Bottom left: After placing a piece of perforated metal over the outlet hole, cover it with a layer of broken crocks. Follow this with a layer of stone chippings.
Top right: Fill the trough with a recommended soil mix and firm well using a brick or similar implement.
Centre right: Group the rock plants before planting and when you are satisfied with the arrangement, begin to set them in the soil, firming each one in as you go.
Bottom right: Pieces of stone are used to create a miniaturised, natural-looking landscape.

If you are just starting with rock plants I would suggest you begin with sturdy, grow-anywhere specimens which will fend for themselves quite happily. You can specialise later if you get more ambitious. In the meantime, choose from alpine dianthus, phlox, saxifrage and sempervivum, *Oxalis adenophylla*, *Armeria caespitosa*, sweet-smelling thymes, and the enchanting tiny campanulas and violas. For a more interesting variety of line and shape, plant saponaria and *Dryas octopetala* to climb over the edges and soften them prettily, and add a dwarf tree or bush, perhaps *Chamaecyparis obtusa nana*, or the Noah's Ark juniper, *Juniperus communis compressa*, to lend height and proportion.

Finally, don't neglect an underplanting of tiny bulbs. Species crocus, chionodoxa, *Iris reticulata* and *I. histrioides*, and the fascinating dwarf daffodils, especially hoop petticoat and angel's tears, are all worth a place in this very special garden.

Coping with the Remainder

The vegetable garden is another work generator that could be made smaller, or given up completely and paved over. On the other hand, a greenhouse is a very pleasant place to potter in, easy on the legs and back and rewarding in the produce it can yield. But it's sensible, if possible, to buy one that almost looks after itself, with self-watering benches, self-operating ventilators, and self-switching, thermostatically controlled heating.

If greenhouse gardening doesn't appeal, you might like to acquire another sort of comfortable refuge in the shape of a small summerhouse or gazebo to grace the lawn now that it's used rather less frequently as a playground.

The growing-old garden should be a restful, companionable place, with several seats in sun and shade, and paths wide enough to walk with a friend, or, if necessary, manoeuvre a wheelchair. Incidentally, the latter will need a gentle ramp to move from one level to another, but otherwise

A greenhouse is the answer to gardening in comfort, especially if it is fitted with some of the automatic devices now available.
Above: The extractor fan looks after ventilation and the electrically heated propagator ensures success with the trickiest operations of rooting cuttings and germinating seeds.
Right: Greenhouse ventilation can be completely automatic, controlled by one of these valves. The main cylinder contains a heat-sensitive fluid which expands or contracts with any changes in temperature and raises or lowers the arm of the ventilator.

shallow steps, preferably with some sort of handrail, are easier for the elderly to negotiate.

Even when you have made all these modifications, the fact remains that the garden is, essentially, a growing thing, and there are some chores which cannot be avoided. Watering is one of the most important and tiring. Make sure that you have at least one easily reached tap or standpipe at a convenient height, and a hose-pipe with a sprinkler attachment, as well as a lightweight, long-spouted watering can.

Below: A lean-to greenhouse built against the kitchen wall and kept well stocked with plants of the season makes a fascinating outlook for anyone working at the sink.

Tools to Make Life Easier

Finally, indulge yourself with any equipment you fancy that will make necessary chores easier. A good power mower is a must, and there are also on the market such splendid tools as an automatic hoe; a spade specially designed for gardeners who cannot bend; a long-handled trowel; and flower-gatherer secateurs which both cut and hold the flowers; a 'grab' to pick up leaves, hedge-trimmings and garden refuse; a kneeler which combines with a stool. All of these make life much easier.

When your garden has been planned, and planted, for practicability, and provided with well-designed labour-saving equipment, it will continue to be a constant delight well into ripe old age.

Left: The kneeler-stool is a boon for the elderly and, indeed, for younger people who like to take their gardening in easy stages.
Right: Some additions to the range of tools mentioned earlier will help to make life easier for the less active. Shown here are a selection of long-handled hand tools which do away bending, and a 'grab' which can be used to pick up garden refuse and leaves.

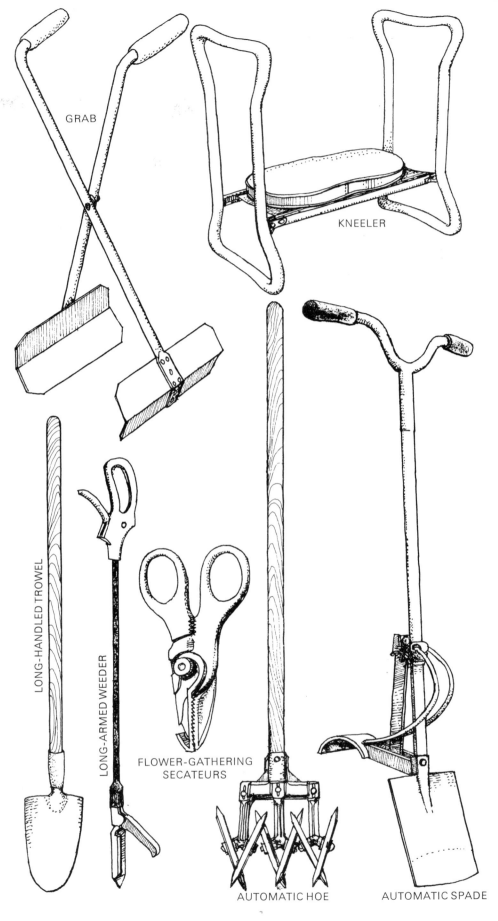

GRAB

KNEELER

LONG-HANDLED TROWEL

LONG-ARMED WEEDER

FLOWER-GATHERING SECATEURS

AUTOMATIC HOE

AUTOMATIC SPADE

Gardens, New and Old

Depending on the sort of house or flat you live in, your garden will be either brand new, or second-hand. In my gardening years I have had to cope with both sorts and have discovered that each has a balance sheet evenly divided between the asset and the debit columns.

Below: A modern garden which has been designed with ease of maintenance in mind. Interesting features include the circular lawn and large plant containers set in pebbles.

A New Garden

Without a doubt, a new garden constitutes a great deal of hard, physical labour to get it into shape.

If the builders have left it looking like a waste-land, the first job is to clear it of debris and dig all of it over, omitting only those areas that are to be paved or pathed or built upon. Don't throw away all the broken bricks and stones – they'll come in useful as the hard core to make the base of a terrace or patio. And don't do the digging by hand if you can avoid it. You'll almost certainly find a mechanical cultivator for hire if you ask around or place an advertisement in your local paper or corner shop, and this will be money well spent on a genuine time- and labour-saver.

By the time you have cleared and turned over the soil you will, no doubt, have a good idea of its nature and condition, and will be coming to some conclusions about what you would like to grow in it. But before you plant, *plan*.

Work out exactly how much space you've got and how you can use it for the maximum benefit of the whole family. It's a good idea to draw a scale map of the garden on a piece of paper, then cut out various shapes to represent lawns, flowerbeds, terracing, paths, and so on, and to move them around until you've achieved the most pleasing combination.

Unless you have a passion for formality, straight lines are to be avoided. A winding path is almost always more inviting than a straight one, but it must lead to something – a seat, perhaps, or a bird table. Curve the edges of your lawn too, and make your beds and borders oval, circular or fan shaped. Gentle lines are not only more soothing to the eye – they also lend an air of mystery by making it impossible to see everything at one glance. The loveliest gardens always have one or two secrets.

Where you want privacy or shelter provide yourself with fencing and grow a beautiful climber up it. If you have an ugly view, block it off with a screen of fast-growing trees. The Lawson's cypress, *Chamaecyparis lawsoniana* Green Hedger which rapidly reaches 4·5 m (15 ft) is invaluable for this, easy and sturdy; the Leyland cypress, *Cupressocyparis leylandii* is another quick mover and a good choice for a fast-growing hedge.

Probably you will prefer to have your kitchen garden away from the house, with a tool shed nearby, but the herb garden and greenhouse should be as near the kitchen door as possible although not in any shadows cast by the building.

Do use at least one of the flowerbeds near the house as a winter garden (page 114) so that you have the pleasure of seeing beautiful things growing and blossoming in the worst months of the year without leaving the comfort of your living room. You might also like to position a scented border (page 111) near the doors and windows so that its perfume welcomes your visitors and pervades the house on warm days and summer evenings.

Many simple ideas can be picked up from this small town garden.

63

While the soil is settling you can make your patio and paths, using materials to suit your taste and purse. You'll probably choose either concrete, coloured for a softer effect, or paving, square or 'crazy', for the patio. For paths, the choice is more extensive, and can include asphalt/bitumen, brick, gravel, stone chippings or grass. Grass is cheap, easy and lovely to look at, but it is less hard-wearing, requires more upkeep, and doesn't dry out as quickly. All the other types of path will need the occasional application of weedkiller to keep them tidy.

Now it's time to start growing things. Begin with the lawn (see page 35), and if you can possibly afford it, grow it from turves rather than grass seed which not only takes a long time to give a durable surface, but also involves weeks of battling with both the elements and the birds. Too much rain, and the seed gets washed away. Too little, and it refuses to grow. And even if the weather is perfect, the birds, which you have fed so lovingly during the lean months, think this is a special picnic, just for their benefit. And there's no reasoning with them. Not even fearsome scarecrows and festoons of tinkling tinfoil can change their fixed conviction that your lawn seed is their bean feast. The only solution is a covering network of stretched black threads. That really thwarts

Above: Set stepping stones into the lawn at a slightly lower level to enable easy mowing.
Right: To break up an area of paving set water-washed pebbles into mortar, levelling them with a board and spirit level.

them, and is a must if you choose this method of making a lawn.

Next, turn your attention to flower-beds and borders, starting at the back with fencing plants and tall growers, and working gradually to the edge, finishing off with little rockery plants and tiny bulbs. If you are planning to underplant with ground cover, remember that you must put these into clean, weed-free soil if they are to do their job properly. It is a complete, though comforting, fallacy that ground-cover plants smother and kill established weeds. All they do is discourage seedling-weeds from growing up through them, and even then they sometimes lose the battle. When planting shrubs and perennials, remember that most of them will spread out very rapidly, so leave plenty of space around them. This will look bare to start with but the spaces can always be filled temporarily with a few informal clumps of bedding plants or annuals.

And now, choose a tree. No garden is complete without one provided that it is the right size for its environment. It would look lovely growing in the lawn, underplanted with spring bulbs. Select a specimen that has already grown reasonably sturdy so that it won't take too long to look established.

Finally, plant up your kitchen garden. Fruit and vegetable growing can be a time-consuming business, so start with just a few rows of ubiquitous easy-growers that are family favourites and will freeze happily if you get a glut. Once your new garden is complete and thriving there will be time to expand and experiment.

Laying a path
Top right: Put in guidelines and dig out a trench.
Top far right: Firm in rubble.
Centre right: Rake over a layer of sand and check level.
Centre far right: Place five dots of mortar on level surface.
Bottom right: Set slabs onto mortar.
Bottom far right: Tap paving slab level with a pick axe. Finally check alignment with a spirit level.

An Instant Garden

Grass turves, well-grown trees, container-grown shrubs and perennials, and budding bedding plants can all combine to give instant results in new gardens.

Rapidly-growing climbers like the honeysuckles, *Lonicera americana* and *L. halliana*, and the incredibly speedy Russian vine, *Polygonum baldschuanicum*, can give a mature look to fresh fencing and raw walls, and some of the creeping ground-cover plants, such as *Lysimachia nummularia*, lamium and ajuga, will waste no time in filling up bald spaces on the surface of newly cultivated soil.

But the cheapest way to quick summer flowers is by means of hardy annuals. A rough plot of sunny land can be transformed in a matter of about two months while you are waiting to begin your permanent planting.

Simply mix together the seeds of colourful easy-to-grow flowers like cornflowers (*Centaurea cyanus*), marigolds (calendula), Californian poppies (eschscholzia) and Shirley poppies (*Papaver rhoeas*) and sow them in far-flung handfuls on the surface of lightly raked soil. Keep them well watered until they are growing strongly, dead-head them after flowering if you can find the time, and you'll have a superb patch of sizzling colour to enchant you for weeks on end.

Stick to two golden rules when you are stocking your garden, and you can't go wrong.

1. Grow only those plants that are right for its own special situation, climate and soil, and, of these
2. Grow only those plants that you love, either for their looks, their scent or their flavour, or for some particular function, such as attracting bees and butterflies.

When there is such richness to choose from, why waste time and space on anything else?

Pyrus salicifolia pendula is a most suitable tree for the smaller garden. It may eventually reach a height of about 7·5 m (25 ft), but its weeping habit and grey-green foliage make it a favourite.

A Second-hand Garden

If you inherit a second-hand garden two other golden rules apply.
1. Be patient, and then
2. Be ruthless.

If you can bear it, you should live with an established garden for a complete year before you do anything to it apart from minimum maintenance.

During the twelve months, make a note of which plant grows where, when it flowers, what colour it is, if it is healthy and flourishing, and, most important, whether or not you like it.

At the end of that time, harden your heart and get rid of anything you don't like. You may be able to donate superfluous plants to friends and neighbours with different tastes, or find a jumble sale or charity bazaar with a garden stall. The important thing is to get them out of your garden, even if they end up in the dustbin. I once spent years living reluctantly with red-hot pokers (kniphofia) which I loathed, just because it seemed unfeeling to cut them down in their prime. The relief I felt when I eventually went berserk and totally annihilated them can only be compared with that gained by a delayed visit to the dentist for the removal of an aching tooth. Oh, the joy, when I gazed upon that yawning gap in the border!

Trees are the most permanent occupants of the garden and should be chosen with care. Consider the height, shape of the head and colour of the foliage when making your selection.

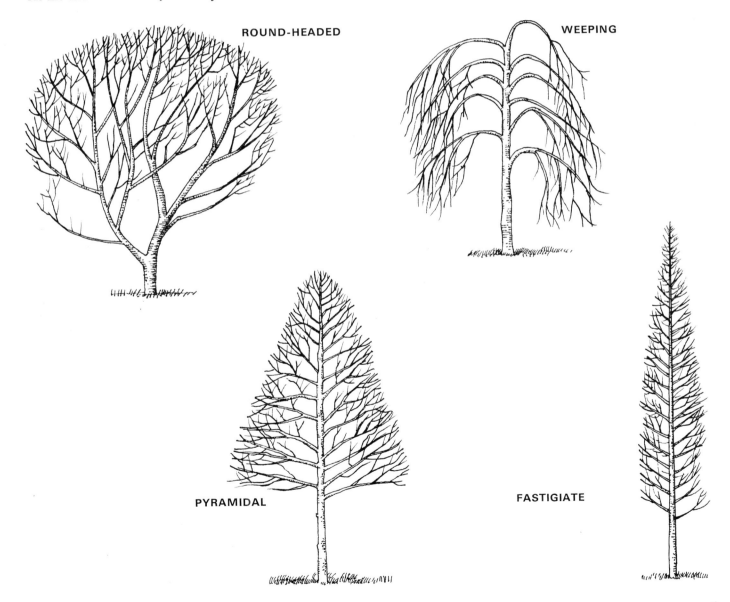

ROUND-HEADED

WEEPING

PYRAMIDAL

FASTIGIATE

I would even advise you to eliminate old trees if they have got out of hand. A horsechestnut is a joy and a delight – but not in a cottage garden. Many people feel that they have some sort of solemn duty to preserve trees, but if they have grown too big and become quite out of proportion they can be an absolute menace. They rob the house of light, they keep the sun from the garden and they drain the soil of food and moisture. So, if you have a tree and you don't like it, consider the possibility of chopping it down. The stump can be turned into a very pretty garden by filling its crannies and hol-lowed trunk with pockets of soil and planting it with tiny flowers. And then you can replace the giant with some-thing more dainty – perhaps the lovely willow-leaved pear, *Pyrus salicifolia pendula*, or a neat Japanese maple, like *Acer palmatum dissectum*, especially the purple-leaved variety. My own in-stinct would be to steer clear of the cherries and laburnums. Beautiful they most certainly are, but so widely grown nowadays that they have be-come something of a gardening cliché. It's much more rewarding to choose something a little different.

It may well be that in your garden-

One common fault in tree planting is to place the tree too close to the house, so that when it reaches its full height, all or part of the house is in shadow throughout the year. So check the aspect and ultimate height of the tree and position it accordingly, giving due regard to the angle of the sun in both summer and winter.

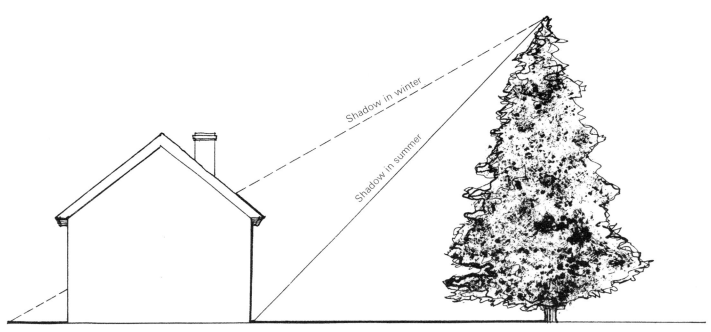

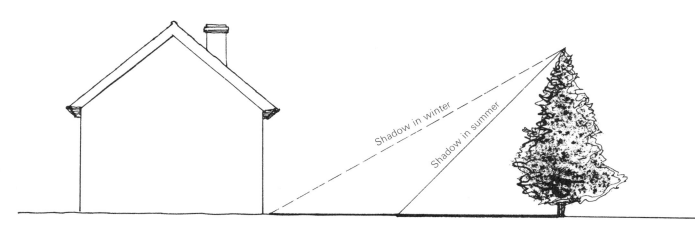

ing sabbatical you will have found other plants and shrubs which are the right things for you, but in the wrong places. You will also have discovered that a garden planned for another family doesn't measure up to the requirements of your own.

If so, change it. It's not a good idea to make do or try to compromise. You will never be satisfied with the results, and the garden will never seem completely your own. So make your alterations, but be gradual. Make them one at a time so that the rest of the garden can be lived in and enjoyed even while it is being re-created.

Paths are basically a permanent feature so you will probably prefer to leave them alone unless they are disastrously wrong. But it is a very simple matter to alter the shape and position of lawns and planted areas. Turves, for instance, can easily be lifted from one place and moved to another without damage. Perennials, bushes and even small trees can be transplanted quite safely during the autumn and winter provided that the weather is not frosty or the ground too dry. A patio or paving can be laid on what was originally planted soil if a firm base of hard core is put down first of all.

However, if you have acquired a shed, conservatory or greenhouse which is not wanted, think very hard before you demolish it. If your aversion is caused by its ugliness it will be easier to beautify it than pull it down. Fresh paint and an overcoat of climbers, or a screen of tall flowers supported against trellising, will work wonders.

If the offending article looks all right but doesn't seem appropriate for any job you might want it to do, you can probably modify it to suit your family's life-style.

You may not want to garden in a greenhouse, for instance, but, provided with blinds or shuttering, it could become a marvellously light studio. Or you could remove what is left of the glass, plant it up on the outside and transform it into a fabulous pergola.

A traditional conservatory might seem like hard work, but it could be very useful as a toddlers' playroom, or a toy, games and bicycle store.

A garden shed made redundant by a capacious garage could take on new life as a splendid dark room for a budding photographer, a Wendy house, a den, a hobbies or games room, or a quiet study.

With buildings, especially if built upon solid foundations, it's usually much wiser – and more fun – to restore and renovate rather than remove.

Garden eyesores can often be transformed into attractive features. For example, an old tree stump can be planted with flowers, and a greenhouse no longer wanted can be covered with attractive climbers and used as a summer house.

Making the Most of a Small Plot

Tiny gardens obviously need rather different treatment from those composed of proud and spacious acres. They certainly present more of a challenge. But there's no reason at all why they shouldn't be just as beautiful as the larger ones.

When planning on a minor scale, four rules should be borne in mind.

1. Choose only small and dainty plants in strict proportion to the space available.
2. Consider the third dimension, and include walls and fences as part of the growing space.
3. Extend your limited area by using containers of all sorts – urns, tubs, troughs, growing-bags, hanging baskets, window boxes, and so on – and
4. Deceive the eye of the beholder whenever possible.

A tiny garden is the place for neat-growing shrubs, dwarf perennials, alpine plants, species bulbs, low or prostrate herbs, and a single, dainty tree, preferably fastigiate, weeping or trained against a wall. If these are kept in careful proportion to each other they will create the illusion that they are much bigger – and that therefore the garden is much bigger – than is actually the case.

Opposite: A garden in which full use has been made of all available space. The tiered beds offer a massed bank of colour which cannot otherwise be contrived in such a small space.

Selected Plants for the Small Garden

Shrubs:
Daphne mezereum, Hebes in variety, Helianthemum in variety, *Hypericum calycinum* (Rose of Sharon), *Lavandula spica* Hidcote, *Mahonia fortunei*, *Potentilla fruticosa* hybrids, Rosemary, *Santolina chamaecyparissus*, *Senecio laxifolius*.

Perennials:
Achillea (dwarf varieties), Asters (including dwarf Michaelmas daisies), Aquilegia, Delphinium (dwarf varieties), Dicentra, Geranium (cranesbill), Phlox, Pulmonaria, Solidago (dwarf varieties), Trollius.

Alpines:
Armeria, Aster (alpine), Aubrieta, Campanula, Dianthus, Perennial Iberis, Phlox (alpine), Primula (alpine), Saxifrage, *Viola gracilis*.

Bulbs:
Winter aconite, Species anemone, Chionodoxa, Species crocus, Erythronium, *Galanthus nivalis* (snowdrop), Muscari, Miniature narcissi, Puschkinia, Scilla.

Herbs:
Asperula (woodruff), Chamomile, Chives, *Mentha requienii*, Thyme.

Trees:
An espalier-trained apple or pear, *Betula pendula youngii* (weeping birch), *Chamaecyparis lawsoniana fletcheri* (Lawson's cypress), *Prunus* Amanogawa (columnar cherry), *Pyrus salicifolia pendula* (willow-leaved pear).

If you can't find room for a small tree you could have a container-grown tree instead. A bay tree in a tub looks elegant by a front door – one at either side looks even better. Pot-planted standard roses have a formal charm about them which makes them admirably suited to town houses, as do some of the small junipers and cypresses.

In a minute garden there is really no place for a separate fruit and vegetable plot, but that doesn't mean there is no place for fruit and vegetables. The solution is to plant them either in mixed beds and borders, or in containers.

Runner beans and runner French beans can easily be grown up walls, bean-poles or a wigwam of canes as a decorative feature. Asparagus peas and alpine strawberries can be used either as ground cover or edging plants. The tiny lettuce, Tom Thumb, will thrive quite happily along the front of a border, rhubarb can serve as a background foliage plant, and cucumbers and courgettes can either be allowed to drape over the edge of steps or trained up trellising.

Strawberries, the Zeva raspberry, and tomatoes, especially the bush varieties and the tiny, decorative currant types, will flourish in barrels, pots and window boxes, and a collection of herbs is both attractive and useful in a planter, or simply in a varied assortment of plant pots arranged near the kitchen window-sill or doorstep.

Climbing Plants are Important

If you grow plants *upwards*, on trellises, fences, walls or posts, you obviously get much more greenery and flowers per square foot than if you grow them on the ground, so climbers are a must for the restricted garden. Fortunately, there are so many to choose from that it is possible to have something in flower, fruit or berry for most of the year.

Roses are indispensable and are discussed later, see page 94. Two clematis I wouldn't be without are the early and incredibly easy *montana*, and the late summer *tangutica* which has pretty, silky seedheads as well as lovely yellow flowers – I can never understand why it isn't more widely grown. Neither of these needs much pruning, simply the removal of dead or weak wood after the flowers are spent or the seedheads withered.

The honeysuckles are a must too – in a small garden their scent will permeate to every corner and fill the house whenever a door or window is left open. *Lonicera japonica halliana* is the one I would choose, since it is evergreen and flowers from early summer well into the winter months. It does, however, tend to make a take-over bid for the entire garden if you turn your back on it for one moment. The popular

Why not dress up the front door with a pair of bay trees in tubs or, if the house is away from the road and out of temptation, a pair of container-grown fruit trees.

gardening term 'invasive', is a euphemism where this one is concerned, so be ruthless, harden your heart, and hack it back mercilessly the minute it gets too big for its boots.

The climbing hydrangea, *petiolaris*, is useful too, since it is self-supporting and will happily cover a chilly shaded wall shunned by more tender specimens. This one is yet another plant which deserves to be more popular than it is.

Finally, try to find some wall space for *Jasminum nudiflorum*, so delicately beautiful, yet one of the first to flower, and therefore twice as welcome as the later, showier forsythia which waits until the daffodils are in bloom to produce its own store of gold.

Incidentally, don't be inhibited about double planting, using one plant as a host for another. Clematis, for instance, will twine happily among roses to bloom among their branches, and roses, wisteria and nasturtiums will wander up old trees without causing any damage and with doubled beauty.

Below left: Clever use of paving and raised beds makes the most of a small space.
Below: It is equally important to utilise any wall or fence and few climbers are better for this purpose than clematis.

Planting a container

Top row: Make sure the container has adequate drainage holes. Then put in a layer of pebbles to a depth of about 5 cm (2 in) and fill the container with a suitable potting compost such as John Innes Potting Compost No. 2.

Bottom row: Firm down compost well using a brick. Plant firmly working from the centre outwards to the rim. Finally water the plants in well.

A planted up container is illustrated on the opposite page.

Containers Are a Must

If your garden is short of growing space – or if, in fact, your growing space is in the wrong place, in dense shade, perhaps, or a very exposed situation – the answer is to grow things in containers.

Practically anything can be container grown, provided that care is taken to make sure that it is adequately drained, watered and fed.

What's more, practically any receptacle can become a plant container. There are lovely ones on the market – Ali Baba pots, stone urns, teak troughs and tubs, wrought iron hanging baskets, terra-cotta jardinières. The choice is endless – and expensive. But there's no need to spend money. You probably have dozens of potential containers in cupboard, attic or garden shed just crying out for a face lift and a new role in life. From chamber pot to kitchen sink, paint tin to pie dish, biscuit box to burst bucket, there's no limit to the possibilities.

When making a choice all you need to do is match the size of the container to the potential, or required, size of the plant. If the container is too small the plant will become root-bound and its growth restricted.

Plants for Containers

Bulbs:
Species crocus, Daffodils, Galanthus (snowdrop), Hyacinths, *Iris reticulata*, Muscari, Scilla, Lily-flowered Tulips.

Annuals:
Centaurea cyanus (cornflowers), Eschscholzia (Californian poppies), *Matthiola bicornis* (night-scented stock), Nasturtiums.

Summer-bedding Plants:
Ageratum, Antirrhinum, Begonias, Calendula, Callistephus (china aster), Heliotrope, Lobelia (trailing), *Matthiola annua* (ten-week stock), Nemesia, Pelargoniums, Petunias, Tagetes.

Shrubs:
Azaleas, Camellias, Fuchsias, Hortensia hydrangeas.

The easiest container of all these days is the ubiquitous and labour-saving growing-bag which can be bought in sizes large or small, already filled with compost, complete with instructions, and ready for planting. They make ideal homes for tomato plants, runner beans, cucumbers, melons, courgettes, peppers, aubergines, lettuce, strawberries, a collection of herbs, bedding plants like geraniums and petunias, and most other flowers. They seem to me to be absolutely fool-proof, and I use them with a hundred per cent success every year. Now it's also possible to buy a climbing frame to fit them, so stakes and strings are a thing of the past for tomatoes or climbers.

The main and continuous concern when gardening in growing-bags must be *never* to neglect the watering. When the plants are growing vigorously, especially in hot, sunny weather, each bag might need as much as 7 litres ($1\frac{1}{2}$ gallons) a day, so if you go on holiday do persuade a friendly neighbour to take over this chore for you in return for a share of the crop.

Growing-bags can seem expensive to buy, since they can only be used once, but shop around and the chances are you'll find them for sale at less than the manufacturer's recommended retail price. When this happens, snap them up – you've got yourself a bargain.

Don't limit yourself to standing your containers on the ground – they can be positioned at various levels to add visual interest. Growing-bags, as well as troughs and tubs, can be placed at the edges of a flight of steps, on balconies and patios, on flat roofs or walls, while smaller pots look charming on broad, level window ledges.

Among the commercially produced containers, I particularly like hanging baskets. They can look lovely suspended from eaves or porches, above windows, among the branches of trees or on brackets jutting from the walls. But they must always be easily accessible and removable. There's only one thoroughly effective way to water a hanging basket, and that is to take it down every day and immerse it in a bucket for a good long soak of not less than ten minutes.

To plant a hanging basket, first line it with damp sphagnum moss, or with turves used grass-side out, then fill with compost and firm down. Plant the edges with trailers like lobelia and nasturtiums, and ivy, then work in towards the centre, using geraniums or fuchsias, petunias, begonias and verbena.

If you would prefer something different, plant your basket with herbs and hang it near the kitchen. Or fill it with spring bulbs, planting some to grow out through the sides as you would do with a crocus pot.

The smallest garden I know is made up basically of a brick wall and a lot of plant pots. Sturdy shelves have been fixed to the wall, a very broad one at the bottom, a narrow one at the top and those between carefully graduated. Each shelf carries a row of plant

Planting a hanging basket
Top row: Line the basket with moss and begin to fill with a good compost such as John Innes Potting Compost No. 2. Plant the sides of the basket as you go, so the plants trail downwards naturally.
Bottom row: Plant up the centre first, to give height to the arrangement, and then work outwards to the rim. Finally water the completed basket and hang in place.

pots, big ones at the bottom, tiny ones at the top, and these are all filled with a profusion of colourful flowers, dwarf tomato plants, herbs and climbers, some of which trail down while others are trained upwards. As a finishing touch, one or two seedlings of wallflowers, thrift, pinks and aubrietas have been popped into little crannies and flourish gaily among the pots. So simple – yet so effective that passing cars pull up to have a closer look at it!

Visual Effects

Plants in proportion, plants growing up into the air instead of sideways across the ground, plants in a multitude of containers – all these are space-stretchers for the tiny garden. And so is a bit of outright visual trickery.

Mirrors, for instance, work marvels. A long wardrobe mirror fastened to a wall, its back sealed to keep out the damp, its edges framed by greenery to disguise them, can look like an enticing doorway into a linked garden. Smaller ones give the illusion of being tanta-

lising windows. Take care to situate them so that they reflect something that makes it well worth seeing double – a beautiful tree, perhaps, or a flowering shrub.

You could try a bit of false perspective too. A path that narrows as it leaves you deceives your eyes into thinking that its other end is much further away than it really is. Another good idea is to curve the path and to hide its farthest point behind a bush or clump of flowers so that the casual observer has no idea that it has reached the end of its journey. Simple tricks these, that any novice artist recognises, but few gardeners think about applying them practically to extend their visual space.

Learn from the artist about the constructive use of colour too. Plant deep, dark colours, especially blues and greens, at the limits and edges of your plot, and fill the centre and foreground with pale or bright shades, and you will create a beautiful illusion of depth and distance.

A cheerful and attractive effect can be created in a confined space. Here a window box and containers have been carefully planted with climbing and trailing plants to make this pavement garden particularly pleasant.

What Plants to Grow

A Herb Garden

Every keen cook will require the garden to provide a few fresh herbs, and many of these are very easy to grow.

In fact, a herb collection including such marvellous standbys as basil, chives, lemon balm, marjoram, parsley, sage and thyme doesn't even need a garden. It can be very happily housed in pots on the kitchen window-sill, in a trough or window box, or planted in a barrel with holes around the sides.

However, most herbs will grow better in the open garden, so if you can spare the space and time to make a herb plot near the kitchen door it is well worth it.

In general, herbs need a dry, light soil and a sunny situation to bring out their maximum flavour. An exception is the mint family which enjoys a fairly heavy, moist soil. Mint also needs to have its roots contained, perhaps in an old, bottomless bucket – otherwise it will rampage madly all over the garden.

Two or three plants of each variety of the herbs of your choice should be planted to make sure that you have enough to use, fresh, dried or frozen, in a multitude of ways, from scenting the linen to pepping up the stew.

Plant tall growers at the back, or in the centre if it's an island bed, put the smaller ones towards the edges, and underplant with creepers, like thyme, just as if you were planning a mixed border. Remember to give them plenty of space, for most of them will develop into spreading or bushy plants and do not take kindly to crowding. And if you are concentrating on saving labour stick to perennials, the boon of the busy gardener.

As far as flavour is concerned, perennial herbs are at their best in the early summer, so harvest some then for freezing, or making into herb butter.

Keeping Herbs

There are various methods of freezing. A good one is to sprinkle the chopped leaves into the ice-cube tray of your refrigerator, and fill it with water. When they are frozen, the herb-cubes can be stored in polythene bags, and are simply used by adding one or two to casseroles, soups and so on when required.

Alternatively, you can pack the chopped herbs separately into air-tight containers or foil envelopes, using them straight from the freezer by crumbling out as much as you want, when and where it's needed.

Another possibility is to prepare a number of *bouquets garnis* by making up bunches of two or three sprigs of parsley, one of marjoram, another of thyme and a bay leaf. Pack them into an air-tight container, freeze and use one at a time when required.

For drying, gather the herbs on a dry and sunny day just as their flowers are opening. Snip off dead and damaged leaves, then make them up into small bunches. These should be hung in a warm, dry, airy place until they are brittle. Some of the more succulent herbs, such as mints, parsley and fennel, can be spread out thinly on paper and dried in a warm oven.

When thoroughly dried out, pack the bunches into polythene bags, fastened tightly, and store them in a dry place. Remember that just a pinch of dried herbs can give a very strong flavour, so go carefully when you're cooking with them.

BAY

MINT

The Good Cook's Top Ten for the Herb Garden

BALM:
Sow seed indoors at the beginning of summer. Plant out in ordinary light soil in a warm sunny position, when the seedlings are 8 to 10 cm (3 to 4 in) high.

Alternatively, plant roots in the open garden, or in deep containers, either in spring or autumn.

Used in stuffings and sauces for a lemon flavour, in salads, in fruit salads, and with poultry and veal. It also makes a good herb tea.

BASIL:
Grow basil from seed sown under glass in late spring, and transplant after about six weeks on to light, rich soil in a situation that is warm, sheltered and sunny.

A good flavouring for pizzas and pastas. It is tasty sprinkled on beans and courgettes, and particularly delicious with all tomato dishes.

CHIVES:
Either grow from seed sown in the spring on rich, well-drained soil with plenty of sunshine, or plant a clump of chives bought from a nurseryman.

Chop finely and add to salads, sauces and soups for a mild onion flavour. Very good blended in butter, or added to scrambled eggs, meat balls, welsh rarebit, omelettes, and mashed potatoes.

FENNEL:
Grow fennel in a sunny spot from seed sown in early spring.

Use chopped like parsley in salads, especially sprinkled on cucumber. Or blend into a white sauce to serve with fish. The tender stems, cut before flowering, can be peeled and served with vinaigrette sauce as an accompaniment to tinned fish.

GARLIC:
Plant cloves of garlic in early spring, about 13 cm (5 in) apart. They like rich soil and an open, sunny position.

Use dried and powdered, blended into butter. Slivers pushed into the surface of roasting meat bring out the flavour and act as a tenderiser. Whole cloves, rather than chopped ones, add a subtle taste to stews and casseroles. Garlic vinegar, made by adding 55 g (2 oz) skinned and chopped cloves to 570 ml (1 pint) of white vinegar, is a delicious addition to salad dressings.

MARJORAM:
Sow seeds out of doors in late spring in shallow drills of well-fertilised loamy soil, where they will get lots of sunshine.

This herb makes a tasty flavouring for soups, casseroles, stews, stuffings, omelettes, herb butters, cottage cheese, and salads. It also makes a good garnish for Brussels sprouts, cabbage, cauliflower, carrots, mushrooms and courgettes.

MINTS: *including Apple, Eau de Cologne, Peppermint, Pennyroyal, Spearmint, Pineapple, etc.*
All mints like a moist, rich soil, and a partially-shaded position. The usual way to grow them is from roots planted out in the spring. Mint is a rampant grower and spreads rapidly, so confine the roots in a bottomless bucket.

This is in many ways one of the most useful of all herbs. The best mint sauce is made from a combination of both spearmint and apple mint in equal parts. Pineapple mint is good in fruit salads, soft drinks, and jellies. Eau de Cologne mint makes a delicious flavouring for an orange or lemon jelly, is a good tea, and is tasty with peas. Pennyroyal is the best to sprinkle on new potatoes or to make herb butter, and most of them can be chopped with parsley to add to scrambled eggs.

ROSEMARY:
It is possible to grow rosemary from seed, but it is much easier to buy a young plant about 30 cm (1 ft) high. Propagate either by layering, or by stem cuttings taken in late spring and summer and then planted out in well-drained soil in a sunny, dry position.

A sprig placed on any roasting joint adds to its flavour. With a joint of lamb, prick holes over the surface at 5-cm (2-in) intervals and insert individual leaves. Rosemary tea is refreshing, and good for headaches. You could also try rosemary conserve, either spread on bread, or as an alternative to redcurrant jelly to serve with meat dishes. It is made by beating up the freshly cut tops with three times their weight in honey. A sprig of rosemary added to the cooking water gives flavour to old potatoes.

SAGE:
Start sage from seed sown in mid-spring in shallow drills. It will flourish in poor soil provided that it gets plenty of sun. It can easily be propagated by layering, cuttings or root-division.

As well as being a familiar ingredient of stuffings and sauces to accompany rich meats, sage is an excellent flavouring for cottage or cream cheese, or for herb butter. Sage tea is a good remedy for digestive upsets and for sore throats, and can be used externally to bathe bruises and sprains.

THYME:
In the middle of spring sow the seeds where they are to grow, choosing a sunny plot of light, rich soil.

Use widely as a good flavouring for soups, stews, casseroles, stuffings, minces, egg dishes, salads, and as a garnish for leeks, broad beans, carrots, onions, courgettes and aubergines. Rub a joint of beef with the leaves, and sprinkle some over the top for roasting. It's also good with poultry and baked fish, and makes savoury herb butter and cheese.

Herb Butter

This is delicious, and can be made with fresh, frozen or dried chopped herbs. Quantities for fresh herbs are as follows: to 225 g (8 oz) of butter add 2 tablespoons of chives, 4 teaspoons of parsley, 1 teaspoon of chopped marjoram, 4 cloves of garlic, crushed, and salt and pepper, and blend well. If dried or frozen herbs are used you will need less. Some of the butter, which is superb with French bread, can be frozen for later use. A small pat thrown on to vegetables just before serving will give them a delicious flavour. Different combinations of herbs can be used according to personal taste – chives on their own are very good.

Unusual Ways with Herbs

Of course, there's no need to restrict herbs to savoury dishes and salads. They can make delicious desserts and drinks. For instance, mint leaves make a superb sorbet with which to finish a meal.

Mint Sorbet

Boil together 140 ml (¼ pint) of water with 110 g (4 oz) of sugar for three minutes, and then allow to cool. Wash a handful of mint leaves, add the syrup to them, blend them together, then strain through a nylon sieve. Add the juice of a lemon, pour into an ice-tray and freeze for about an hour. Return it to the blender, beat well and fold in 2 stiffly beaten egg whites. Pour into a plastic container and freeze, removing it about 15 minutes before serving.

Herb Teas

Also called 'tisanes', these are very refreshing and pleasant to taste. Use 1 teaspoon of fresh or dried herbs for each person and one for the pot, which must on no account be a metal one. Pour over freshly boiling water and let it infuse for 5 minutes before serving, then add sugar to taste. Lemon balm, bergamot, mint, rosemary and German chamomile are all good. Another interesting tisane is made from dried strawberry, raspberry or blackberry leaves mixed with an equal amount of peppermint and thyme.

The petals and flowers of many herbs, especially borage and rosemary, can be candied, or frozen in ice-cubes, in the same way as those of roses (page 99).

Herbs can be useful for beauty care too. Did you know, for instance, that rosemary tea is a good skin tonic? That the juice pressed from parsley counteracts freckles, and sage, thyme, and rosemary are all good for your hair, encouraging growth and making it shine? Simply boil a handful of the leaves of the herb of your choice in a little water, strain it and use it as a final rinse.

Other Uses for Herbs

Many families like to have their herbs growing together in a garden all to themselves, but this is not necessary of course. In fact it probably makes for easier gardening – though not necessarily easier cooking – to incorporate the herbs of your choice into the mixed border and the vegetable garden. It is a fact worth knowing that many herbs can be very beneficial to other garden plants if they are allowed to grow side by side, and if plants are prepared to look after each other you might as well let them. After all, it's all the less work for you.

Rosemary, sage, lavender, mints and basil, while growing, are fragrantly beautiful, natural insecticides, keeping all kinds of damaging insects at bay. Dried and finely crumbled, and with an addition of dried, powdered garlic, they can be sprinkled on seeds as they are sown, before they are covered with soil, and will protect them from seed-eating creatures right from the beginning. Continue sprinkling with powdered garlic at the seedling stage and birds and insects will steer clear. In the same way both ants and rats will be discouraged by pennyroyal mint.

Incidentally, if you hang baskets of mixed mints above your doors and windows, the chances are you will receive less visitations from passing flies to whom their smell is anathema.

In the kitchen garden,
Tomato plants benefit by the presence of borage, basil, marigolds and parsley.
Potatoes and strawberries benefit from borage.
Asparagus benefits from parsley and chamomile.
Cabbages benefit from sage, mint, thyme, rosemary and chamomile.

The most universally valuable of these herbs are chamomile and marigolds. In fact, chamomile is frequently referred to as a 'physician plant' since it is widely used by gardeners to strengthen sickly young plants growing nearby. The marigold, as well as being so colourful, is phenomenally useful. To start with, it is a weedkiller, helping to control ground ivy, horsetail, couch grass and ground elder; secondly, it kills off damaging nematodes in the soil, and thirdly, it is an effective insect repellent. Choose the Africa marigold, or *Tagetes erecta*, and plant it far and wide for a healthy and happy garden.

But for culinary purposes, the pot marigold, *Calendula officinalis*, is the one. Its petals can be used in salads, in savoury sandwiches, sprinkled on egg mayonnaise. They can be used as a substitute for saffron, and as a seasoning for sea-food.

Right: Herbs have many varied uses. Herb butters can be made by creaming together softened butter and freshly chopped herbs of your choice; they make a delicious accompaniment to fish dishes. Herb vinegar adds a sparkle to salad dressings. It is simple to make, just add a sprig of any herb, such as tarragon or thyme, to a bottle of wine or cider vinegar.

A Kitchen Garden

Unless you have a massive family of hungry mouths to feed, I wouldn't suggest that you stock your kitchen garden with common vegetables chosen for crop quantity rather than quality – you can find plenty of those in the supermarket. The busy family gardener should have two main aims – maximum flavour, minimum labour.

So think carefully about what you are going to plant. For instance, if you see a dwarf variety give it due consideration. Staking-up can be both troublesome and time-consuming.

My own choice for the kitchen garden includes early potatoes, the most delicious variety I can find; peas and beans, including the less obvious varieties; salad stuffs; courgettes; rhubarb; several soft fruits; and an espalier-trained apple tree.

To get the best out of your fruit and vegetables they should be planted in an open, sunny site where they can grow in fertile, well-drained soil. Good thorough digging and manuring before planting is vital for a substantial harvest. I'm afraid you must be prepared for the fact that a kitchen plot *does* involve more work than a flower-bed, but you can console yourself with the comfortable thought that, with food prices rising daily, time spent here equals money in the bank.

Vegetables

Potatoes

Quite apart from the delicious taste of a good early potato like Arran Pilot, this vegetable is a great asset to the gardener working on a new or neglected plot. It will do quite well in soil overrun with difficult perennial weeds, and by the time it has been grown and lifted it will have broken up the earth so thoroughly that the weeds will be easy to remove. Consequently, for the following season, the ground will be clean and well prepared for a crop of peas or beans or whatever else you choose to plant there.

Plant early potatoes at the beginning of the spring as soon as the worst of the winter is over, in a spot where they will get the most sunshine. You will know when the crop is ready because the leaves will begin to die down. Lift on as fine a day as possible, when the soil is quite dry. Use a fork, and keep it well away from the centre of the plant so that the potatoes will not get damaged.

New potatoes do not freeze well but they will keep if placed on a bed of straw and stored in a frost-proof building away from the light which will make them green and dangerous to eat. Some can be kept for a long time if they are laid in dry peat in tin boxes and buried in the garden. But don't forget where you've put them!

Potato Salad

Here's a deliciously different potato salad that your family might enjoy. Mix chopped banana sprinkled with lemon juice with diced apple, pine-apple, cucumber, celery and cold, cooked potatoes. Add whipped cream and a little french dressing, stir well and serve with cold, cooked ham or chicken.

EARLY POTATOES
Plant out: In early March, placing the tubers 30 cm (12 in) apart in trenches 13 cm (5 in) deep. Leave 60 cm (2 ft) between rows.
Harvest: In June or July, the time for lifting usually corresponds with flowering.

Peas

These are an all-time favourite, especially with children, but it's a good idea, I think, to choose dwarf varieties, especially a good tasty 'early' like Little Marvel, which will only need minimal support. Again, they are a helpful plant in that they leave behind them a soil enriched with nitrogen. It's a wise gardener who, after the harvest is gathered, chops up the old plants and returns them to the soil or put them on the compost heap.

For the best possible flavour, pick your peas when they are very young and sweet. You'll find that any surplus will freeze beautifully.

Do take the trouble to plant some of the less common types of pea as well, finding room for cobri, asparagus and sugar peas. *Cobri peas*, or petit pois, have an excellent flavour provided that the pods are picked early before the seeds are full-size. The plants grow about 1 m (3 ft) high, and are very heavy croppers. The best way to cook the peas is to steam them in their pods, which can be easily removed when they are ready for eating. Serve with butter and chopped mint.

In the case of both sugar and asparagus peas, the pods are eaten along with the seeds. The *sugar pea*, which is a small 'mangetout', will grow only about 45 cm (1½ ft) high, and will give an abundance of pods during late summer.

The *asparagus pea* grows so well in a warm, sunny, sheltered spot that it doesn't need to be confined to the kitchen garden. It can even be used as ground cover in the mixed border, or make an edging to a path where its pretty red flowers form an attractive feature. Its winged pods should be gathered when they are just over 2·5 cm (1 in) long, then steamed in a very little salted water for about ten minutes and served with melted butter and black pepper. Don't overcook them or they will lose their delicate flavour. They make a very nutritious dish served on their own, with brown bread and butter, and are quite economical, since one packet of seeds should provide more than enough for a family of four throughout the summer.

As an unexpected bonus it is said that the ripe, dried peas can be ground and used as a coffee substitute. I haven't been brave enough to try it yet, but if world coffee prices keep on rising I certainly will.

To freeze pod peas, wash well and remove both ends and any strings. Blanch for half a minute in small quantities so that they remain crisp, chill quickly, and pack in polythene bags or boxes. Cobri peas are better eaten fresh.

PEAS
Sow: From March to June, 8 cm (3 in) apart in a 5-cm (2-in) deep trench. An early crop can be obtained if the seeds are started off in February under glass.
Support: With hazel twigs or canes and string.
Harvest: Pick the peas young and pick them regularly.

ASPARAGUS PEAS
Sow: Under glass or indoors in April 1 cm (½ in) deep in seed trays.
Plant out: End of May or beginning of June, 38 cm (15 in) apart in the row.
Support: Allow plants to sprawl, or place canes either side of the row with twine stretched between them.
Harvest: It is important to pick the pods when they are young and tender, or they will become stringy and lose their delicate flavour.

Beans

Dwarf French beans are an invaluable addition to the kitchen garden, providing a good supply of vegetables from midsummer for about three months, and adding a rich flavour to summer meals. There are many varieties to choose from, some of them, like the mauve-coloured Royalty, as good to look at as they are to eat. They flourish in a sunny bed of rich soil, but cannot withstand frost, so if they are sown early they must be protected. Keep the plants well-watered in dry weather, and pick the pods regularly when they are young.

To cook them, wash, top and tail the pods, and cut into 5-cm (2-in) lengths. Boil for 5 to 10 minutes in salted water, strain and pour cold water through them, then simmer gently in herb butter for 10 to 15 minutes.

If you want to save space, and have a sunny wall or fence, you might prefer to plant climbing French beans there, against netting for support. French beans don't drop their flowers as runner beans do, so every one should pod. Gather these when they are about 15 cm (6 in) long, and don't worry too much if they fill out before you get to them – they are unlikely to get as stringy as runner beans.

Runner beans are not, in my estimation, as tasty or tender as French beans, but they do tend to provide a bigger harvest for a longer period, as well as looking rather handsome against a wall or trellising. They can be used to disguise an ugly building too, or to hide a view of dustbins or compost heap. Scarlet Emperor is a good choice. Or you could try a dwarf runner instead. Hammond's Dwarf Scarlet is only 45 cm (18 in) tall, and therefore an easy one to manage. It does not need a support and can be allowed to trail on the ground.

You should get three months' provision of beans from your runners from late summer onwards.

To freeze runner beans and French beans, trim off the ends, wash them, blanch for two minutes, drain, cool and freeze in polythene bags.

Alternatively, if picked when young, they can be salted down and kept for a period of up to two years. Slice them, place a layer in a storage jar and cover with salt, add another layer, and so on until the jar is filled. When they are needed, remove the required amount, wash free of salt, soak for an hour or two, then cook by steaming for about an hour with a covering of butter and a sprinkling of herbs.

FRENCH BEANS

Sow: Singly in pots in March or April indoors or under glass. Sow outdoors from May to July, 5 cm (2 in) deep, 15 cm (6 in) apart.

Plant out: In May, allowing 20 cm (8 in) between plants and 45 cm (18 in) between rows.

Harvest: As soon as the beans are large enough to use. Pick regularly.

RUNNER BEANS

Sow: In April indoors or under glass singly in pots, or at the end of May outdoors 5 cm (2 in) deep and 30 cm (12 in) apart.

Plant out: At the end of May, spacing plants 30 cm (12 in) apart.

Training: Train plants up poles or nets, nipping out the growing tips of the beans as they reach the top of the supports.

Harvest: Pick over every few days from July to September to keep the supply of beans coming on.

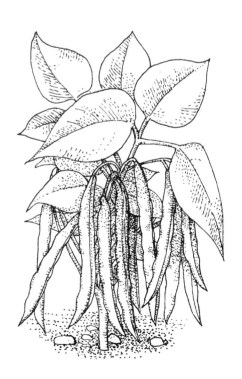

Turnips

Turnips are often looked down upon as the poor relation of the vegetable garden, but if they are pulled young, when no larger than a tennis ball, they are sweet and tender. Choose the summer turnip, Early Snowball, sow it in spring between rows of peas, and it should be ready for picking in less than three months.

This one is well worth freezing. Trim it, peel it, dice it, blanch it for two and a half minutes, cool it and pack it in a rigid container.

Courgettes

Courgettes, both green and gold, are becoming more and more popular in our gardens and kitchens; and rightly so, for they make an attractive plant with their interesting yellow flowers, are easy to grow, very prolific, and good to eat *if* they are harvested at the right time, before they get too large, and cooked properly.

Courgettes are easy to grow from either seed or young plants put out in the garden in early summer. Give them a sunny position in good moisture-retaining soil, allowing each one 1 to 1·25 m (3 or 4 ft) of space. Pick the fruits when they are 8 cm (3 in) long – don't let them get bigger or they will lose flavour. Fortunately, the more you pick, the more you'll get. To keep a family supplied regularly throughout the summer allow one plant for each person.

To cook courgettes, wash them, top and tail them, slice into a pan and simmer in butter for ten minutes. Alternatively, halve them longways, season with salt and pepper, sauté in butter until they are tender, then lay them side by side in an oven-proof dish, sprinkle with grated cheese and cook in a moderate oven for about twenty minutes.

Many cook-books will tell you that it's perfectly all right to freeze courgettes, but I have never found that it works very effectively. My advice would be to use them and enjoy them as you pick them.

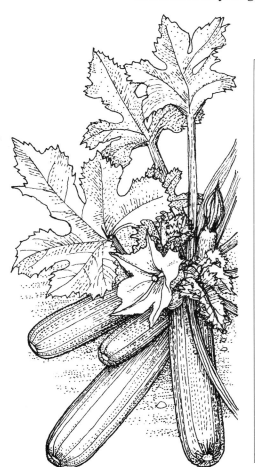

TURNIPS

Sow: Outdoors from February until August about 2·5 cm (1 in) deep.
Thin: When the seedlings are large enough to handle to leave 15 cm (6 in) between plants.
Harvest: About three months after sowing, from June until November.

COURGETTES

Sow: Indoors or under glass in April. Sow one seed on edge in each 8-cm (3-in) pot.
Plant out: At the end of May or the beginning of June. Plant into moisture-retaining soil that has been enriched with plenty of well-rotted manure or compost.
Training: The trailing types will happily ramp over the whole garden if left to their own devices. It is best to train them up a post or trellis, then with careful stopping and pinching out the laterals they can be kept under control. Alternatively, grow the bush varieties which do not involve so much work.
Harvest: Young tender courgettes can be picked from the end of June until the beginning of October. The fruits are at their best when they are about 8–10 cm (3–4 in) long.

Salads

Tomatoes

There have been revolutionary developments as far as tomato-growing is concerned which make them, at last, perfectly possible for the labour-saving garden.

Now you can grow tomatoes out of doors even in cold, exposed areas, and get ripe fruit from them even after a bad summer. What is more, there are many bush varieties available, The Amateur, for instance, which need neither 'stopping' nor staking.

There are also very attractive dwarf tomatoes, like Tiny Tim and Pixie, which grow less than 60 cm (2 ft) high and are ideally suited to growing in tubs on the patio, or at the edge of a path. They yield tiny, sweet tomatoes which should be served whole.

Sadly, the tomato plants you'll find for sale are usually the more ordinary varieties, though this may change in time if demand keeps up. If you feel unable to face the fiddle of raising tomatoes from seed you will be stuck with what your nurseryman wants to sell you, and they will probably be the sort that need staking.

In this case, the easiest way to grow them – in my own experience – is in a proprietary grow-bag, supported by a specially designed frame made for this very purpose. The main chores will be pinching out the side shoots, weekly feeding, and copious watering, but the rewards, in the shape of pounds and pounds of perfectly fresh tomatoes, will be well worth it. In fact, grow-bags are an absolute boon to busy gardeners, especially those struggling with difficult soil, tricky growing conditions or lack of space.

Creamed Tomatoes

If you prefer your tomatoes cooked rather than raw, try creaming them as an accompaniment to poultry, meat or fish. Skin 450 g (1 lb) of tomatoes, chop them and dredge with seasoned flour. Put them into a frying pan with 55 g (2 oz) of butter, and sprinkle with one tablespoon of brown sugar and one tablespoon of basil. Season with salt and pepper, cook very quickly for about ten minutes until the liquid has almost evaporated, stir in 140 ml ($\frac{1}{4}$ pint) of double cream and serve.

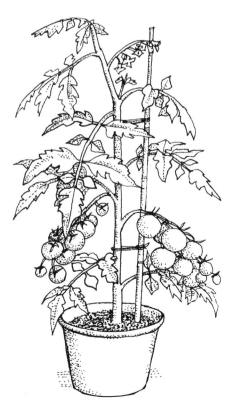

TOMATOES

Sow: From February to April indoors or under glass, a day-time temperature of about 16°C (60°F) and a night-time temperature of about 13°C (55°F) are required.

Plant out: Pot up plants individually when the seed leaves have opened out. Transplant out of doors at the end of May or the beginning of June into containers or growing bags.

Training: Bush varieties need no special training; other kinds should be trained up sticks or string for support and should have their lateral shoots pinched out as soon as they appear. These plants should also be stopped after 4 or 5 trusses have set.

Spacing: Leave at least 45 cm (18 in) between plants.

Harvest: From May to October depending on where the plants have been grown. Green tomatoes can be made into chutney or ripened on a windowsill or in a box lined with paper.

Lettuce

A row of lettuce is a must in the kitchen garden, easy to grow, and providing fresh, wholesome food for a long period of the year if several varieties are planted in succession.

The lettuce Suzan can be grown out of doors all the year round if it is given some protection during harsh weather. Put some in the mixed border if you want to save space or fill a gap, but find room in the vegetable plot for delicious Buttercrunch which will stay crisp right through the the summer, and for the huge and tasty Salad Bowl.

Two problems with lettuce. One – it tends to provide you with more than you can comfortably cope with at any one time. Two – given half a chance, it bolts.

Don't despair. Either way, there is a good method of using it up. It makes an extraordinarily good soup, which can be frozen, so there's no need to waste as much as a lettuce leaf.

Lettuce Soup

For a large lettuce weighing about 340 g ($\frac{3}{4}$ lb) you will need one medium onion, 25 g (1 oz) of butter, two level tablespoons of flour, 425 ml ($\frac{3}{4}$ pint) of chicken stock, 425 ml ($\frac{3}{4}$ pint) of milk and seasoning. Slice the onion and cook gently in the butter for a few moments. Add the lettuce, coarsely shredded, cover and simmer for about five minutes. Sprinkle in the flour, pour on the boiling stock and milk and stir until the soup comes to the boil. Then season, put on the lid and cook over a gentle heat for about twenty minutes. Finally, liquidise, or pass through a nylon sieve, for a creamy, unusual dish with a flavour as subtle and delicate as that of asparagus – a favourite with all my family.

Cucumbers

Ridge cucumbers are another invaluable asset in the summer garden, for they are perfectly hardy, and so prolific that at the height of the season the fruits need to be picked daily. Give them a sunny position, but preferably one with some protection from winds. If you are short of space they'll do very well in a tub or grow-bag.

If your climate is mild, and your garden sheltered, you could experiment with the Japanese climbing cucumber which will grow upright against a sunny wall or trellis, and go on fruiting until the first frosts of autumn.

Cucumbers are usually eaten raw and are, of course, very good sliced or diced in salads, either as they are or dressed with plain yoghurt or sour cream. But they can be made into soup, or cooked as a tasty and unusual vegetable to serve with fish or egg dishes and once cooked they can easily be frozen.

Braised Cucumber

Peel two cucumbers, cut into quarters longways, discard the seeds, then cut into cubes. Put these into a bowl, sprinkle with salt, a few drops of wine vinegar and a little sugar. Leave to stand for half an hour, then drain off the liquid.

Put the pieces on an oven-proof dish, sprinkle with two tablespoons of chopped chives, then dot with butter, cook in a hot oven for half an hour and serve.

LETTUCE
Sow: From March to August outdoors in shallow drills 30 cm (12 in) apart.
Thin: To leave 15–20 cm (6–8 in) between plants.
Harvest: Between June and October according to variety.
RIDGE CUCUMBER
Sow: In April indoors or under glass.
Plant out: End of May or beginning of June allowing 60 cm (2 ft) between plants.
Harvest: From July to September.

A Few Fruits

Strawberries

During my long, love–hate relationship with strawberries, I have found them land-hungry plants which attract birds and slugs and need an inordinate amount of looking after. And then, after all that, if the sun doesn't shine at precisely the right time they repay my devotion, hard work and precious garden space by rotting before they ripen.

So, I've given up planting them out in my garden. Instead, I have a strawberry barrel. In fact, I have two – one for the ordinary varieties such as Talisman or Cambridge Premier, the other is planted with the smaller alpine strawberries.

To prepare a strawberry barrel

1. Bore several drainage holes in the bottom of the container.
2. Put in an 8-cm (3-in) layer of broken crocks at the bottom.
3. Put in a second layer, this time of turves turned grass-side down.
4. Fill the tub with fresh loam which should include some moist peat and decayed manure if possible, adding a handful of bonemeal and another of sulphate of potash. When this has settled it should be not less than 5 cm (2 in) below the top of the barrel for easy watering.
5. Plant the strawberries during the autumn, one in each hole, and two or three 15 cm (6 in) apart in the top, for fruiting the following summer. The earlier they

If you haven't the space to grow strawberries in the garden, try to find room for a strawberry barrel. The numbers refer to the stages described on this page.

are planted in the autumn, the better they will fruit the next year.

6. Keep the barrel well watered.
7. Give an occasional feed of liquid manure after the fruit has set.
8. Finally, remember that borage is good for strawberries, and try to have one or two plants growing near your barrel.

Of the alpine strawberries, one that does particularly well in barrels is the old favourite, Baron Solemacher. Unlike their larger cousins, alpines need partial shade. They are for the most part very hardy, less troublesome to grow and less attractive to birds. Since they throw out no runners the best way of propagating them is to divide up the crowns.

If a strawberry barrel seems too much like hard work, you can still grow the alpine kind, very easily, as decorative edging for paths or the mixed border. Alternate the red ones with Alpine Yellow for a spectacular show that is as good to look at as it is to eat.

Try this Strawberry Cup for a warm summer evening.

Strawberry Cup
Mash and sieve about 255 g ($\frac{1}{2}$ lb) of strawberries to a pulp, add about one dessertspoon of brandy – more or less according to taste – and leave to stand for half an hour. To the pulp add an equal quantity of water, the juice and grated rind of one lemon and sweeten to taste. Stir until the sugar dissolves, then strain and serve with a flower ice-cube floating in the glass.

Raspberries

These are easy to grow, give their crop when most of the strawberries are over, taste as good, freeze better and make excellent jams and pies. Try mixing them with mint for an interesting flavour.

One problem though – they don't like chalk, so if you have a chalky garden choose the variety called Zeva and grow it in a container.

Blackberries

Blackberries, of the same family, are similarly easy and delightful fruits, sharing all the same virtues, and extending the soft fruit season well into the autumn since they are not at all troubled by frost. This is very useful since they can be used as an alternative to raspberries in almost all recipes when there are no raspberries left. They also make superb wine, especially Himalaya Giant which, with its large thorns, can be used to make an impenetrable garden hedge.

Like raspberries, they fruit on one-year-old canes, so the spent and weak ones should be cut to the ground after fruiting, but apart from this they need very little care.

Gooseberries

These are becoming quite rare – in fact, in some countries they are hardly grown at all nowadays on a commercial basis. For this reason, I think gardeners should always try to find room for at least one or two bushes.

They are a useful fruit since they thrive in cold conditions, will do well in partial shade and produce good crops without much pruning. What's more, if they are well looked after they will last for thirty years or more. Watch out for the caterpillars of the Gooseberry Sawfly in late spring – they can reduce the foliage to shreds in a matter of days if not picked off and killed.

Some varieties have a rather sharp flavour, but other varieties, like Langley Gage and Thumper, are sweet and juicy.

Many cooks deplore time spent in topping and tailing gooseberries, admittedly a boring and irritating job which holds little charm. The answer is to make dishes like mousses, fools and ice-creams where they can be used as a purée, making topping and tailing unnecessary, rather than tarts and crumbles where it can't be avoided.

Below: Pruning a newly planted gooseberry bush. This is best done in November after planting. Cut back all shoots by about half, to an outward-facing bud.
Below right: Pruning an established bush. First remove any dead, diseased or congested growth, then tip back remaining branches as shown. This is best carried out in February.

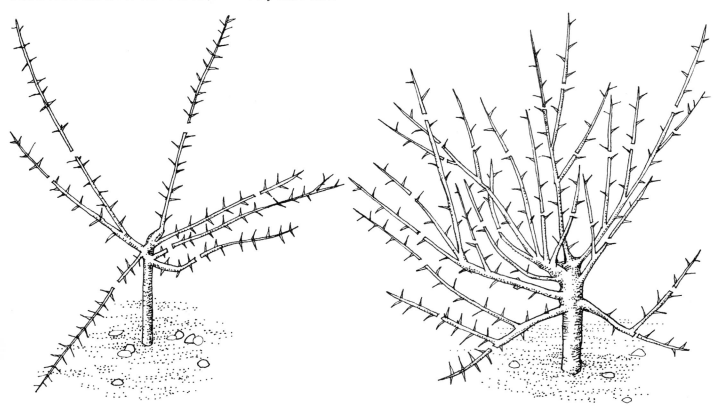

Rhubarb

This, too, is a marvellous standby for the cook's garden. Just as blackberries give the last taste of summer, so rhubarb gives the first – a fresh, zesty tang which heralds all the good things in store.

It is perennial, can be grown on most soils, is acceptable either in the kitchen garden or mixed border, and if pulled young and tender is a splendid economical filling for puddings and pies as well as all manner of other good things.

Choose a good early variety like Champagne, cover its roots snugly in a sacking blanket during hard weather, and you'll have it ready in your garden while prices are still sky high in the shops.

For children who baulk at its rather astringent flavour, stewed rhubarb can be made more bland and acceptable by the addition of a little cornflour.

Apple and Pears

And for the final touch, why not buy an espalier-trained apple or pear tree to grow against a warm, sheltered, sunny wall or fence? All you need is a spread of 3 to 4·5 m (10 to 15 ft), with good, well-drained soil. The trees can be bought with 2-tier or 3-tier branches growing horizontally, and these need to be supported on wires stretched across the surface of the wall or fence at 30-cm (1-ft) intervals.

Make sure when you buy your tree that you are given pruning instructions to help you keep it in shape.

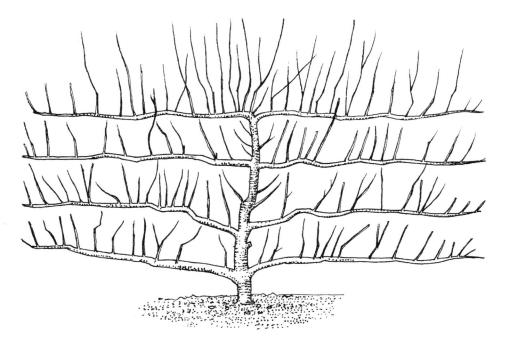

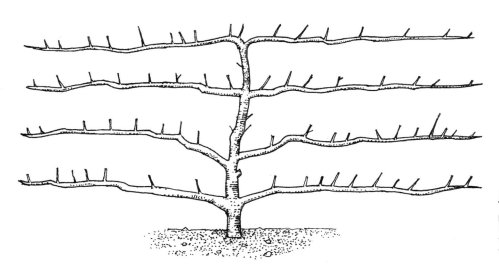

Pruning an espalier-grown apple or pear
Top: Established espalier-trained tree before pruning showing vigorous growth of laterals.
Bottom: Prune in winter by cutting back the laterals to two buds. Leave any potential fruiting spurs unpruned.

93

Some Specialities

Roses for Every Garden

I love roses, and can't imagine living happily in a garden without any. However, from my own family garden I exclude formal rose beds, and banish hybrid teas, floribundas and standard roses. In their place I grow a few ramblers, a lot of climbers and as many shrub roses as I have space for. For the most part these take less caring for than bedding roses, and blend much more happily with other plants, flourishing in mixed borders, thriving against walls and buildings, and making beautiful, impenetrable hedges.

Shrubs and climbers, you will find, need less pruning, and are less prone to pests and diseases than the hybrid teas and floribundas.

Below: Zéphirine Drouhin, trained up the front of a house, wafts its fragrance indoors each time the door or window is opened.
Right: The beautiful shrub rose *Rosa mundi* is an asset to any garden.

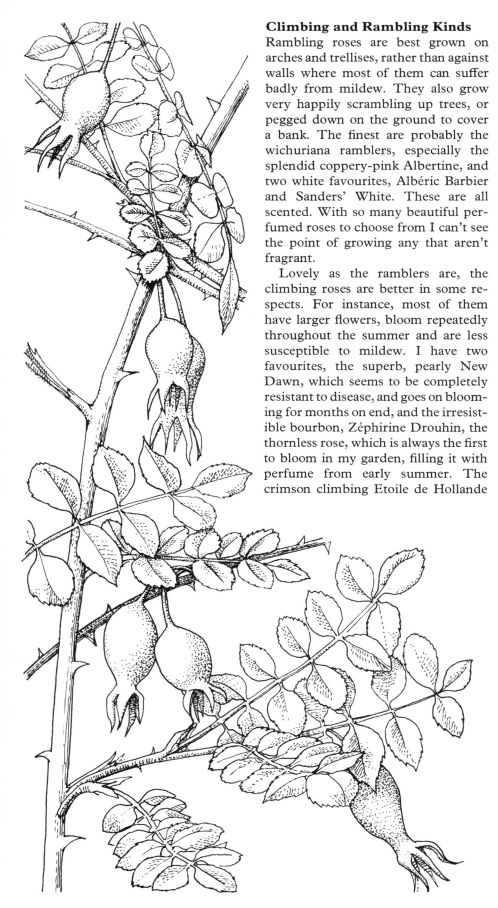

Climbing and Rambling Kinds

Rambling roses are best grown on arches and trellises, rather than against walls where most of them can suffer badly from mildew. They also grow very happily scrambling up trees, or pegged down on the ground to cover a bank. The finest are probably the wichuriana ramblers, especially the splendid coppery-pink Albertine, and two white favourites, Albéric Barbier and Sanders' White. These are all scented. With so many beautiful perfumed roses to choose from I can't see the point of growing any that aren't fragrant.

Lovely as the ramblers are, the climbing roses are better in some respects. For instance, most of them have larger flowers, bloom repeatedly throughout the summer and are less susceptible to mildew. I have two favourites, the superb, pearly New Dawn, which seems to be completely resistant to disease, and goes on blooming for months on end, and the irresistible bourbon, Zéphirine Drouhin, the thornless rose, which is always the first to bloom in my garden, filling it with perfume from early summer. The crimson climbing Etoile de Hollande deserves a place too. It's one of our most beautiful and strongly scented climbers, looks magnificent against a grey stone wall and is – quite literally – good enough to eat. Incidentally, the only pruning required by these ramblers and climbers is the removal of old flower heads – unless the hips are valued – and the cutting out of old or unwanted growths. It's rather a matter of common sense than specialist technique, so don't let it frighten you.

Shrub Roses

Shrub roses are much bigger than the hybrid tea or floribunda bushes, but if you have a large flowerbed they make a magnificent show. Some of them, still flourishing, have a fascinating history that goes back into the mists of time. *Rosa gallica officinalis*, the apothecary's rose, is probably the oldest one in cultivation, and used to be widely used commercially for conserves and pot-pourri. It is still well worth growing and using. *Rosa x alba* is very beautiful too, and though it usually flowers only once during the summer it is to be recommended for its strong scent, great vigour and combination of lovely flowers and foliage. The beautiful, blush-pink Céleste is my own favourite.

One of the great joys of the shrub roses is the subtlety of their colouring. Among the lovely hybrid musks, Buff Beauty is a deep apricot yellow, Thisbe, a buff yellow fading to cream, and Moonlight, a pale, creamy lemon. *Rosa moyesii* has flowers of dusky red and the extra bonus of superb hips.

Among the modern shrubs, the bright yellow Canary Bird is a valuable garden plant, particularly since it is one of the earliest to bloom, and the new Fountain, with flowers of blood red, makes a fine show piece.

Shrub roses don't need pruning in the same way as hybrid teas. They should be treated like other shrubs, the main consideration being to clip them to the size and shape required. It's usually quite enough to cut out old shoots which haven't flowered well, and to cut back the others to where strong young growth is starting.

Another significant difference is

that they do not look at their best growing on their own, but should be planted in a mixed border. For a beautiful show, have a spread of climbers at the back, on a wall or fencing, as well as one or two growing up sturdy posts. In front of them plant the shrub roses. Some of the bourbons, centifolias and hybrid perpetuals – for instance, Boule de Neige, Petite de Hollande and Baron Girod de l'Ain – take up less space than the huge modern shrubs, rugosas and hybrid musks, so are more suitable for a smaller garden, but all of them need space.

A Mixed Border

Other shrubs will grow happily and look good alongside shrub roses. Philadelphus and hardy fuchsias are especially well suited to their company. Herbaceous plants will blend well too. I would choose blue agapanthus, peonies, red, white, pink and yellow, and ornamental alliums as well as hostas. Grey- and silver-leafed plants combine particularly well with roses – santolina, *Stachys* Silver Carpet and *Artemisia arborescens* could all have a place here. Finally, don't omit spring bulbs. Species crocus, snowdrops, *Anemone blanda*, *Iris reticulata* and muscari will all give early colour.

A mixed border with roses seems to me a much better idea for a family garden than either a formal rose bed or a herbaceous border, for it will create less work than either.

Roses as Hedges

Roses can also be of great value as hedging plants – many of them are ideally suited to this function. One of the Gallica family, for instance, the pink and white striped *Rosa mundi* – even the name is beautiful – can make a thick hedge, 1 m (3 ft) high, smothered in enchanting butterfly-like flowers for four weeks in the middle of summer. Many of the hybrid musks, especially Penelope, Felicia and Cornelia, are good hedgers, as are the Alba roses, Maiden's Blush in particular. For a very tall hedge the sweet briars Amy Robsart and Meg Merrilies can be planted, brightening the garden with both flowers and hips.

PRUNING A CLIMBING ROSE

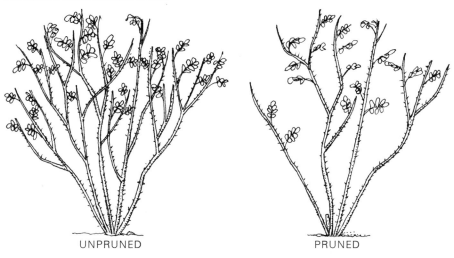

UNPRUNED   PRUNED

PRUNING A LARGE-FLOWERED RAMBLER

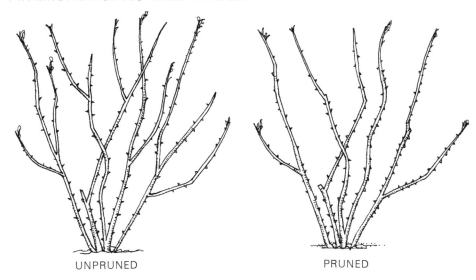

UNPRUNED   PRUNED

PRUNING A SMALL-FLOWERED RAMBLER

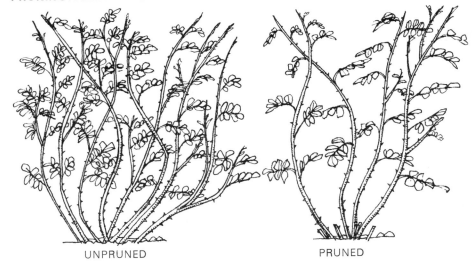

UNPRUNED   PRUNED

The Scent of Roses

The marvellous thing about roses is that they not only look good and smell good, they also taste good and do you good.

The seventeenth-century astrologer-physician, Nicholas Culpeper, devoted several pages of his *Complete Herbal* to the health-giving properties of the rose. Among other things he declared that 'it keeps the bowels regular and is of considerable efficacy for common colds and coughs. Red roses strengthen the heart, the stomach, the liver, and the retentive faculty, mitigate the pains that arise from heat, cool inflammations, procure rest and sleep, and the juice purges and cleanses the body from choler and phlegm.'

I'm no herbalist, but I do know from personal experience that rose vinegar makes a very refreshing skin lotion, and that pads of cotton wool soaked in it and then laid on the forehead do marvels for headaches.

Rose Vinegar

Fill a jar with strongly scented red or pink petals – those of the *Rosa gallica* are especially good. Add white or wine vinegar. Leave it to soak for 24 hours, then strain. Add more petals and let it stand again. Continue this process until the liquid is slightly oily and strongly perfumed, then strain it through muslin and pour into small, tightly stoppered bottles. Keep these in a dark cupboard to preserve the scent.

And how about this fragrant idea from the reign of Elizabeth I?

A Bag To Smell Unto, Or To Cause One To Sleep

Take drie Rose leaves (petals?), keep them close in a glasse which will keep them sweet, then take powder of Mints, powder of Cloves in a grosse powder. Put the same to the Rose leaves, then put all these together in a bag, and take that to bed with you to sleepe, and it is good to smell unto at other times.

Cooking with Roses

I must admit that I do like to eat my roses, and their petals can be used, fresh or dried, in many recipes. Some of the ideas are very simple. For instance, fresh rose petals, chopped up and mixed with other edible flowers, like marigolds, nasturtiums and borage, make an attractive and tasty garnish for a salad. Powdered dried petals can decorate desserts and summer sweets. Fresh dark red petals are a good filling for sandwiches, especially with cream, or cream cheese, and brown bread. A rosebud, frozen inside an ice-cube, gives a glamorous finishing touch to a chilled fruit cup. Or you could try drying three cups of fresh red petals in a cool oven, and then blending them into a pound of unsalted butter. After three days it will have absorbed their flavour and fragrance, and taste delicious. Some can be stored in the freezer to bring the taste of summer into the depths of winter.

Here are a few more rose recipes you might like to try.

Rose Petal Conserve

Take about 25 full-blown scented red roses – Etoile de Hollande is good – and cut off and discard the white heels of the petals, for these are bitter.

Boil together 570 ml (1 pint) of water and 675 kg (1½ lb) of sugar until it is slightly thick. Add the juice of a small lemon, and the rose petals. Simmer for an hour, stirring very frequently, then turn into small pots and cover when cold.

Candied Rose Petals

Pick the petals when the flowers are fully open. Beat the white of an egg until it is creamy then brush it over the petals. Dust them with sifted granulated sugar and spread on waxed paper. Leave to dry in a cool place.

Candied petals can be frozen, or kept in airtight tins spread in layers on waxed paper. They make an attractive decoration for cakes or desserts, and children love them as sweets.

Rose and Fruit Salad

Cover the bottom of a serving dish with pink and red rose petals. Mash 4 ripe bananas and add to them an equal quantity of finely chopped dates. Spread this mixture on top of the petals, then cover with rose petal conserve. Just before serving, pour over the juice of 2 oranges, then spread over it a thick layer of clotted or whipped double cream.

Sharbatee Gulab – a Cool Cup

Wash and dry the petals of 5 large, fragrant roses. Place them in a large bowl, and pour over them 2·5 litres (2 quarts) of cold water. Leave them to stand in a cool place, but not a refrigerator, for 4 hours, then strain, and discard the petals. To the rose water add $1\frac{1}{3}$ cups of sugar and $\frac{1}{4}$ cup of lemon juice. Stir well, then add 3 cups of crushed pineapple, tinned or fresh, and pour this mixture on to crushed ice in a glass jug.

Plants which Control Pests

Since I use roses for cooking and eating, and since I like to welcome birds, bees and butterflies into my garden, I make it an absolute rule not to spray them with artificial insecticides and fertilisers. However, my roses are not, as you might imagine, covered with mildew, black spot and greenfly, because I use one of nature's own methods of sorting out its ecological problems – symbiosis. By and large, I find it safer, easier, less time-consuming, less expensive and much more attractive.

The lovely modern shrub rose Nevada has creamy white single flowers in early summer.

Here are some of the secrets I have discovered.

Roses always benefit from being grown with any member of the onion family, from the modest chive to the showy ornamental allium. Not only do the onions control the rose's black spot, they also persuade it to release a stronger perfume. What's more, it seems incredible but it's true that a clove of garlic planted beside each rose will keep it free from greenfly. Prevent it from flowering if you would prefer to do without its strong smell. In very dry weather you must keep the garlic well watered so that the rose can take up its magical root excretions.

Parsley is beneficial to roses as it also helps to repel greenfly. If it's allowed to flower it will attract bees and butterflies into the bargain.

Nettles, soaked in rainwater for two or three weeks, make an excellent, but smelly, natural fertiliser for roses. This concoction is also a good insect repellent. Alternatively, you can make an infusion by covering a handful of nettles with a pint of water and bringing to the boil. Remove from the heat, keep it covered while it cools, strain and dilute with four parts of water to one part of liquid. This will give you a spray against mildew and aphids.

Choose your roses well, plant them in the right place with sympathetic companions, give them a few hours of your time when you can spare it, and they will grow with health and vigour to be the pride of your family garden.

Planting a bare-rooted rose
Top left: Soak the roots in a bucket of water.
Top right: Place the rose in the planting hole and spread out the roots. Make sure it is planted to the same depth as it was growing in the nursery.
Centre left: Replace soil, firming as you go and finally firm well in.
Planting a container-grown rose.
Centre right: Slit the plastic container.
Bottom left: Place in the hole and remove the container. Tease out a few of the roots.
Bottom right: Replace soil around the root ball, firming as you go.

Birds in the Garden

Welcome birds into your garden by planting a few berried bushes. They will be a lively source of interest, especially if the birds are encouraged to nest in a tree or hedge.

BULLFINCH

BLUETIT

THRUSH

SPARROW

GREAT TIT

MALE BLACKBIRD

FEMALE BLACKBIRD

WREN

Just as I look upon my garden as a natural habitat for children, so I think of it as a place where birds and butterflies should be made welcome and encouraged to stay.

Admittedly, birds damage seedlings and young plants, but the pleasure that they bring in song and flight more than compensates for a few chewed-up lettuces and nibbled peas. So protect the crops you value, either by twining black thread around them or by sprinkling the soil nearby with powdered garlic, then turn a blind eye to any other minor depradations. It's all a matter of priorities.

Birds will come to your garden – and some of them will nest there – if you feed them regularly, make sure that they have a constant supply of water, and trees or shrubs to perch in and give them cover and shade.

You could plant one or two berried shrubs and a few special flowers just for them. Berberis is good, either the evergreen *darwinii* with its shining holly-like leaves and orange flowers followed by plum-purple berries, or the deciduous *wilsoniae* which has translucent coral-coloured berries. This bush is the particular favourite of blackbirds. Or you might prefer a red-berried cotoneaster which will attract thrushes, finches and tits. Mistle thrushes will flock to the fruit of the engaging little rowan tree, a favourite in the Scottish countryside because of its legendary power to guard against evil and keep witches and warlocks at bay.

Starlings are very partial to holly berries. Golden King is a useful variety for the small garden, but the golden fruits of the tall Madame Briot are very beautiful and unusual. Honeysuckle is a great bird-favourite too. Blackbirds, tits and warblers will seek it out for its berries.

Many flowers will produce seeds attractive to birds if you allow them to escape your dead-heading routine. Sunflower seeds, for instance, are not only suitable for caged birds, they are also irresistible to tits, finches and other rarer species. Try to find space too for a few cosmos, scabious, antirrhinums, china asters and the lovely, fragrant oenothera, or evening primrose.

During the winter the birds will appreciate a little extra food to supplement their diet, but there's no need to spend a lot of money on expensive packets of goodies from the pet shop. Many kitchen scraps are very good for them – potatoes baked in their jackets, for instance, damaged or over-ripe fruit, bones, nuts, suet, chopped bacon rinds and cheese, as well as bread and cake crumbs which are not really sufficiently nutritious on their own.

Probably the best idea is to make a special bird pudding, and feed them a portion each day.

Bird Pudding

Take peanuts, grated cheese, oatmeal, crumbled cake and any meaty scraps chopped small. Add some bird seed, either gathered or bought, and some chopped nuts, mix together and put into a bowl, then pour over melted fat, using about 225 g ($\frac{1}{2}$ lb) of fat to each 450 g (1 lb) of the mixture. Allow the pudding to set, store it in a cool place and use daily.

If you wish to attract birds into your garden, plant shrubs with brightly-coloured berries:
Below left: Berberis.
Below: Mountain Ash or Rowan (*Sorbus aucuparia*).
Right: Cotoneaster.

A Bird Table

To make sure that the birds get the food instead of the next-door cat it would be sensible to provide a bird table. A flat piece of wood fastened to the top of a cat-proof, smooth pole or iron tube about 1·5 m (5 ft) high would be adequate. As well as putting food on it you could hang nets of nuts and bones from it. It will give you the greatest enjoyment, of course, if you position it within easy view of the windows of either the kitchen or the living room.

A Bird Bath

Birds need water both for drinking and for keeping their feathers functional, so you should supply them with some sort of bird bath. The simplest is an up-turned metal dustbin lid, either propped up on bricks or sunk into the ground. The sunken variety will look prettier, since you can plant little prostrate flowers like Creeping Jenny (*Lysimachia nummularia*) and thyme around the edges, but make sure that it can easily be lifted for regular cleaning and re-filling. You could put some pebbles or small rocks in the lid if you want to make it look more like a natural pool. Place the bird bath in a shady situation, vary the water level from about 2·5 cm (1 in) at the edges to 10 cm (4 in) in the deepest part, always keep it topped up, never allow it to get iced over and it will give you – and the birds – constant pleasure. Many of those mentioned here will become your regular companions, and with luck you'll also attract some of the rarer species to your bird garden.

Having provided the birds with cover, food and water, please, oh please, don't poison them by spraying your garden with harmful insecticides. They have enough of that to contend with in farmed fields where such rigorous pest control is much more defensible than in the average family garden. If you absolutely must use a pesticide to save your crops of fruit and vegetables, try to restrict yourself to natural pyrethrum which will work effectively if you give it time and keep at it, and do no harm to your bird population or any other warm-blooded creatures. On the other hand, you may have to say goodbye to most of your butterflies. That, for me, is too high a price to pay since I consider butterflies even more beautiful than the flowers I grow – a sort of horticultural kinetic art.

Left: Holly berries attract starlings among other birds.
Right: Build a table for the birds, so they can feed without worrying about the local cats.
 A bird bath is greatly appreciated in hot, dry weather.

A Butterfly Sanctuary

If you share this enthusiasm, careful planting can turn your garden into a butterfly sanctuary. You will need to provide not only those flowers which attract them by colour and scent to their rich source of nectar, but also the plants they use for egg-laying.

It's a good idea to have a little patch of ground set aside as a screened 'butterfly nursery', because some of their egg-food plants are not calculated to gladden the gardener's eye. Several of our most colourful butterflies, like the Peacocks, Red Admirals and Small Tortoiseshells, lay *only* on stinging nettles. The Painted Lady has a permanent passion for thistles. The Small Heath and Meadow Brown require a good supply of assorted grasses.

However, some of the other wild flowers commonly used by butterflies are more attractive and can be introduced into the mixed border quite happily, or planted together in a special wild butterfly corner. Include dog violets, bird's foot trefoil, sorrel, hedge mustard, yellow rocket, heathers, gorse and broom, and you have a good chance of attracting the lovely Fritillary butterflies, as well as the Common Blue, the Small Copper, the Orange Tip and the Green-veined White.

It's a common gardening fallacy that white butterflies are pests. Admittedly, the Cabbage White does devour a lot of green leaves, but the Green-veined White, on the other hand, is friend rather than foe, since it feeds on charlock which is the host plant for such nasties as cabbage root fly, turnip flea beetles and club root.

There's obviously no guarantee that all the young butterflies that hatch out on your plants will actually stay in your garden, but if there is an abundance of the flowers that they like they will come back again and again. Their great favourite is buddleia, the butterfly bush. There are many attractive varieties of this, the colour range including not only the familiar purples and mauves, but also white, violet-blue and dark wine-red. Two good ones are the dainty little *davidii nanhoensis*, only 1·5 m (5 ft) tall, and the elegant, weeping *alternifolia*, which can bear tassels of bloom 1 m (3 ft) long. If you are serious about butterflies you must have at least one buddleia in the garden – in the summer it will be covered with as many butterflies as blooms, a mass of shining wings.

Next to buddleia, butterflies like valerian better than anything. Though really a wild flower it makes a splendid border plant, especially the red variety, *Centranthus ruber*. Yet another wonderful butterfly flower is the old garden favourite, hesperis, or sweet rocket, with its fragrant spikes of purple, violet or white. This plant is doubly valuable. It is attractive to all butterflies because of its strong scent and rich

supply of nectar, and its seed-pods provide food for the caterpillars of the elegant Orange Tip.

In fact, butterflies are attracted by very many of our most common garden flowers and flowering shrubs especially those which are highly perfumed, and they seem to prefer the pastel shades – mauves, pinks, whites, yellows and purples – particularly where they are planted in dense patches. In the spring they will flock to a blaze of massed aubrietas and clumps of yellow alyssum. In high summer they will browse on golden sedums, veronica and the Rose of Sharon, *Hypericum calycinum*. In the last warm days of autumn you'll find them hovering drowsily on the sun-splashed heads of Michaelmas daisies and scabious. And wherever they appear, whether in flight, or delicately poised to feed, they can only add to the beauty of the scene.

Incidentally, some seed firms sell packets of mixed butterfly-flower annuals. These can be scattered in drifts on a spare plot of land, or sown in small clumps in established beds and borders. An even prettier idea is to sow them in tubs and pots which can be moved around the garden so that you can take the butterflies with you wherever you go. Or they can be set on a patio, or near windows – perhaps in a hanging basket – where they can be easily seen. This might be a good, and inexpensive, way to begin your butterfly garden if you'd like to start on a small scale.

Planting for Fragrance

It's a great mistake, I think, to concentrate too carefully on the sights of the garden while taking little or no account of its smells.

Scent is extremely significant in our lives. Nothing is more evocative than fragrance, nothing more potent for triggering off memories and associations. And it is particularly important, of course, to people who have failing sight or are completely blind, so it should be considered with special care by those with a 'Growing-old Garden'.

The thoughtful positioning of scented flowers is also vital. They need a sunny sheltered spot where their perfume will linger in the air on a warm, drowsy afternoon or a mild summer's evening. They should also be near doors and windows, by a patio or terrace, at the edges of paths and planted in the crevices of paths. Some could be in movable tubs so that you can carry or push your pot of perfume about the place, and put it beside your deckchair or hammock, while others will flourish fragrantly in window boxes and hanging baskets.

There are, however, one or two delicious plants whose perfume can be too overpowering for planting close to the house or sitting area. Honeysuckle, *Lonicera japonica halliana*, and the mock orange, *Philadelphus coronarius*, fall into this category.

Scented plants occur among perennials and annuals, shrubs, climbers and herbs. Some give their fragrance through their flowers, others have fragrant leaves as well. Some need to be crushed before they give their full bouquet, while others only release it at night. But altogether there are so many that, with careful planting, the garden can smell enchanting the whole year round.

The Fragrant Year
Though we usually associate scent with summer you can have a perfumed garden in the dead of winter by planting any or all of these three lovely winter-flowering shrubs – witch hazel

(*Hamamelis mollis*), winter sweet (*Chimonanthus praecox luteus*) and *Viburnum fragrans*. Sadly, winter sweet needs to be about six years old before it will produce its flowers freely, but if you have the time it is worth waiting for.

Follow these with dainty *Daphne mezereum*, and underplant them all with the most fragrant of the early bulbs which will bloom at the beginning of spring. I would choose two of the tiny irises, *reticulata* and *histrioides*, and the white, honey-scented *Muscari botryoides album*, and then two indispensable narcissi, pheasant's eye, and the lovely little jonquil. Later in the spring the hyacinths and lily of the valley will add their own heady perfume.

Fragrant perennials for the spring time include violets, wallflowers and the heavenly scented purple *Primula auricula* known as dusty miller, one of my own all-time favourites.

By the time summer has arrived there is an abundance of richly scented shrubs and flowers. Two good shrubs to plant against a wall are *Jasminum officinale* with its white perfumed flowers, and the more unusual Moroccan broom, *Cytisus battandieri*, which has large silvery leaves and yellow blooms smelling deliciously of pineapples.

It goes without saying that every scented garden should have its fair share of fragrant roses, lilacs, sweet peas, pinks and carnations. Try to find room too for the strongly perfumed alyssums, especially Snow Carpet and Royal Carpet, herbaceous phlox, sweet-scented stocks and *Centaurea moschata*, sweet sultan.

And grow the scented-leaved pelargoniums for their fragrance, planting them in pots by a door or window where you can easily pick a sprig to enjoy its perfume. Different species of pelargoniums smell of lemons, oranges, apples, almonds, roses and peppermint. They make a most appealing group, despite their neat, unassuming appearance and lack of colour. Since they are not frost hardy they should be brought indoors for the winter months.

Summer-flowering bulbs for your fragrant year come primarily from the lily family, especially the beautiful *Lilium regale*, and the later *Lilium auratum*, the golden-rayed lily of Japan, often described as the queen of the lilies.

For evening perfume night-scented stock is a must, and so is nicotiana, the tobacco plant, especially *Nicotiana affinis*, but I would also plant mirabilis, the Marvel of Peru, and heliotrope, cherry pie, which are both particularly good after a shower of rain.

Many of these flowers will linger on until the autumn if they are looked after and carefully dead-headed, but for extra scent late in the year rely on our old friend, the *halliana* honeysuckle, which will last until the viburnum is in bloom again. There is also a good, strongly scented winter-flowering bush honeysuckle, *Lonicera fragrantissima*, which is an absolute joy in the darkest days of the year.

A Knot Garden

If I were growing herbs primarily for perfume rather than for cooking I would, without a doubt, indulge my fancy with an enchanting knot garden.

Knot gardens are of ancient origin and were great favourites with the first Elizabethans who cultivated, used and valued their herbs prodigiously. It is thought that they got their name from embroidery patterns, and that the gardener was using his herbs in imitation of the way a lady used her silks to create formal patterns.

The knot garden can be of any design of your choice, its shape made up of small hedges and tiny beds of herbs intersected by narrow walk-ways. A beginner might prefer to start with a simple rectangle, but two other easy ones, the wheel and the ladder, are probably more interesting and satisfying.

The most aromatic herbs to plant in clumps in your knot garden include the fragrant-leaved bergamot, *Monarda didyma*, for massing in a bold group, all sorts of mints, Sweet Cicely, *Myrrhis odorata*, with its lacy, fern-like leaves and aniseed flavour, marjoram, *Origanum onites*, lemon balm,

Melissa officinalis, and finally, near the paths, the feathery burnet, sanguisorba, little grown these days but valuable, not only for its scent, but also for its delicate cucumber flavour.

Lavender, rosemary, hyssop and the traditional *Santolina chamaecyparissus* can all be used for little hedges, kept clipped neatly into shape.

For the paths, since you won't expect them to get too much heavy wear, use carpeting herbs, the creeping wild thyme, *Thymus serpyllum*, chamomile, *Anthemis nobilis*, the pennyroyal mint, *Mentha pulegium*, and *Mentha requienii*, all of which actually enjoy being walked upon. Take a tip from the great Elizabethan, Francis Bacon, who wrote, in his essay *Of Gardens*: 'Those flowers which perfume the air most delightfully, not passed by as the rest, but being trodden upon and crushed, are three: that is burnet, wild thyme, and water-mints. Therfore you are to set whole alleys of them, to have the pleasure when you walk or tread.' Don't despair if you can't stretch to 'whole alleys' – a little path will do just as well.

Having grown the most beautifully scented plants you can find, it would be sensible not only to enjoy their fragrance in the garden, or in bowls set about the house, but also to preserve their perfumes to use indoors when their flowering period is over.

One way to do this is to make potpourri. Here is a popular Victorian recipe for it.

Pot-pourri

To a basinful of dried, scented rose petals, add a handful of mixed marjoram, lemon thyme, rosemary and lavender flowers, all well dried. Add the rind of one lemon and one orange, dried and powdered, six crumbled bay leaves, 14 g ($\frac{1}{2}$ oz) of bruised cloves and a teaspoonful of allspice. Mix well together. Keep for the most part in a covered jar that will not let in the light, but when you wish to enjoy its perfume, take off the lid, mix the potpourri well and stand it in a warm place.

Or perhaps you would prefer a herb pillow to lull you to sleep or soothe

away a headache or the stresses of a busy day? It's very easy to make.

Dry equal quantities of aromatic plants – lavender, rosemary, lemon balm, thyme, mint, bergamot and the fragrant pelargoniums, as well as anything else you happen to have grown. Use the leaves only, and add to them a little orange and lemon peel, dried and powdered, a few cloves and a handful of dried parsley.

Pack the mixture into a small, pretty pillow-slip, embroidered, perhaps, with a flowering herb motif. It is now ready to put on your bed, tuck in at the back of your most comfortable armchair, or give to a friend as a charming and unusual gift. Its summer-fresh fragrance will give lasting pleasure the whole year round.

Right: The knot garden can be any design of your choice, its shape made up of small hedges and tiny beds of herbs intersected by narrow paths. A beginner might prefer to start with a simple rectangle, but the wheel and the ladder are easy and probably more interesting and satisfying.

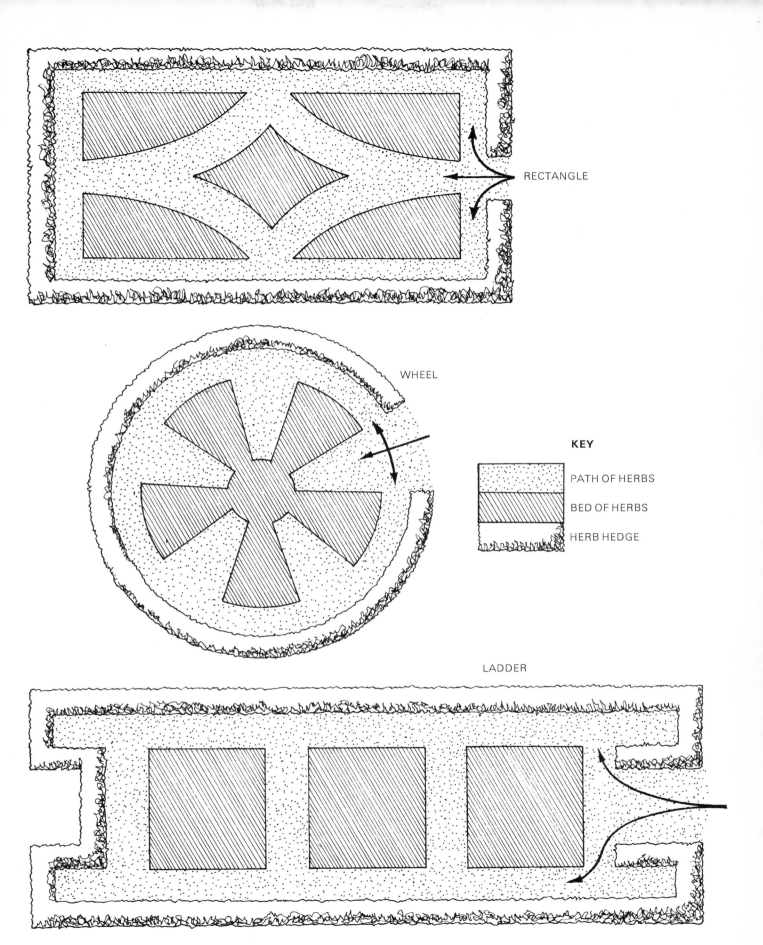

RECTANGLE

WHEEL

KEY

PATH OF HERBS

BED OF HERBS

HERB HEDGE

LADDER

A Winter Border

Even if your garden is very small it would be a shame to consider it merely a place for summer pleasure, with little or nothing to offer during the winter months. In fact, if one of its functions is to provide you with a view from your window, it is perhaps even more important that it should look good during the cold weather when you will have precious little opportunity for actually spending any time out there enjoying open-air activities.

Incidentally, I find that 'winter' is a period difficult to define. It begins and ends at different times in different places. In some years, if the weather is kind, it is short – in others it's endless. And the calendar is no help at all. So, for my present purposes, I've defined winter as the period of time between the withering of the Michaelmas daisies, and the flowering of the larger daffodils.

In some ways, growing things can look even lovelier in winter time. A deciduous tree, for instance, can look more beautiful when it has shed its leaves to reveal the elegant tracery of bare branches beneath. An evergreen shrub often looks much prettier when it is wreathed in glowing berries than when it is bearing comparatively insignificant flowers.

So set aside one part of your plot as a winter garden in which *every* plant has earned its place because of a special winter attraction. Not necessarily winter flowers, of course, though there are plenty of these. There are also plenty of attractive fruits, seedheads and berries, stems, bark and leaves to be taken into consideration.

Choose a corner of the garden which is plainly visible from the windows of the house, and which can easily be reached, even in the murkiest weather, without tramping through mud or wet grass. And try to ensure that it has some shelter from prevailing winds. If there isn't a wall to protect it you might have to plant a hedge, or erect a fence or screening, to hold back the worst of the weather.

It's also a good idea to plant plenty of evergreen ground cover to protect roots and tender shoots from frost and heavy rain. Naked soil is not a particularly good idea in any garden, least of all a winter garden.

Two other precautions. First of all, bear in mind that wet, clayey soil is anathema to winter-flowering plants. If you are gardening on heavy clay, dig in a quantity of grit, rubble and peat for one or two seasons before you begin permanent planting. Secondly, if you are going to want to move around in your winter garden, to pick flowers and stems perhaps, or merely to enjoy its beauty and fragrance at close quarters, it would be wise to position a few stepping stones at convenient places so that you can get about it in bad weather without trampling down the soil and compacting it too severely.

So, now you've found the place, what about the plants? To start with, there are many beautiful winter-flowering shrubs which deserve inclusion. We are familiar with a lot of them already, from earlier chapters – *Viburnum fragrans*, for instance, winter sweet (*Chimonanthus praecox*), witch hazel (*hamamelis*), the winter-flowering bush honeysuckle (*Lonicera fragrantissima*), *Daphne mezereum*, *Jasminum nudiflorum* and *Mahonia japonica*, with its fragrant lemon-yellow flowers. We must include at least one of the winter cherries, too, and my vote would go to *Prunus subhirtella autumnalis rosea*, a real beauty, and tough to boot. And it would be well worth trying something just a little more unusual in the shape of *Garrya elliptica*, a very handsome, large, evergreen shrub with lovely, long grey-green catkins in winter. It needs protection from cold winds, but should do well against a sunny porch or growing up the sheltered side of a building.

Among the berried shrubs, the holly, *Ilex* Golden King, with its gold-edged leaves, *Berberis stenophylla* and *Cotoneaster conspicuus* – or the weeping kind, *Cotoneaster hybridus pendulus* – will bring the birds to your winter garden to double your pleasure. The hips of *Rosa moyesii* Geranium will look quite spectacular, and in the charming *Pernettya mucronata* you will have a splendid show of many-coloured berries, pinks, whites and reds, that will persist all winter. Personally I am not very fond of either skimmia or pyracantha, but they are very rich in winter colour so you may like to include them.

With some shrubs, it's stems that provide the colour rather than flowers or berries. Cornus is particularly exciting, the variety *alba sibirica* is a vivid red, while *stolonifera flaviramea* is bright yellow. Planted together, against evergreens or a pale wall, they can look quite startlingly beautiful, especially rearing up from a dense bed of large-flowered snowdrops. But *never* plant red-stemmed cornus against a red brick wall – that combination spells visual disaster.

If you have room for a tree, the weeping birch, *Betula pendula youngii*, is at its best in winter when its white bark and purplish twigs are most clearly seen, and the mountain ash, *Sorbus aucuparia asplenifolia*, takes on a second beauty, after the glory of its autumn berries and golden leaves, when pale winter sunshine gleams upon the subtle bronzy sheen of its bark. It's an invaluable little tree this one – a thing of beauty the whole year round – so if the garden is only big enough for one tree, this could be the one to choose for all-round usefulness.

And don't forget the evergreens; they, too, look handsome during the winter. They're not all green, either. For instance, Lawson's cypress, *Chamaecyparis lawsoniana erecta aurea*, is tinged with gold, the Irish juniper, *Juniperus communis hibernica*, makes a column of silvery blue-green, while the oriental *Thuja plicata semper-aurescens* forms a big, canary-coloured ball. There are very many to choose from, with a large range of subtle colourings and interesting shapes. Shape is particularly important in winter, of course, when outlines can be seen in stark relief without the summer veil of leaves and flowers that changes the face of the garden.

Helleborus corsicus bears its green flowers from February to April and is doubly attractive when its leaves are edged with frost.

Finally, getting nearer to ground level, there are a surprising number of winter-flowering bulbs and perennials to choose from. As well as snowdrops there are the tiny irises, *reticulata* and *histrioides*, winter aconites, chionodoxas, early flowering crocus, muscari, *dwarf* daffodils as opposed to the miniatures that are better in a rock garden or alpine trough, scillas and *Anemone blanda*, all of which will bloom before the end of winter if you choose your varieties carefully and give them some shelter. Plant with them the beautiful Christmas rose, *Helleborus niger*, but remember that its flowers will have a greater chance of remaining unblemished if you cover them with a simple cloche – a pane of glass propped up on a couple of bricks should do the trick. Add that finest of all the winter-flowering herbaceous

plants – *Iris unguicularis* – which should be given a protected position in full sun then left undisturbed if it is to flourish, as well as honesty and physalis for the silver and flame of their seed-pods. Now all that remains is to plant several clumps of lime-tolerant *Erica carnea* and *E. darleyensis* as colourful ground cover, and you will have created a garden that will be full of brightness, texture and visual interest all winter long.

A White Garden

I have an abiding passion for white flowers, especially scented white flowers. It's not that I don't enjoy colour. I gasp with admiration at the sizzling orange silk of the oriental poppy, I am enchanted by the burning blue of the little alpine gentian, *sino-ornata*, I am intrigued by the subtlety of the pale green moluccella. Nevertheless, my feeling for white flowers can only be described as a passion.

The first flowers that I was ever given, when I was barely sixteen, were white rosebuds. The sender thought he had made a terrible mistake. His friend and adviser, just turned seventeen but already knowledgeable in the ways of women, said that white flowers cost less to buy and were therefore less valued as a gift. He added that, as a token of affection, only red roses would do. He came to the conclusion that the budding romance was doomed to wither before it had even blossomed. But he was wrong on all counts. Five years later I married the boy who had had the good taste to prefer white, and white rosebuds were my wedding bouquet.

Yet the thought of a white garden did not occur to me until I came across the legendary woman gardener, Victoria Sackville-West, and her famous White Garden at Sissinghurst. In her and her gardening philosophy I discovered a woman after my own heart. Rules meant nothing to her. She used plants with the sensitivity and imagination of an artist applying paint to his canvas. And she knew all about the

Below: The cool white flowers of *Clematis montana* clambering over a wooden shelter.
Opposite bottom: The deliciously perfumed *Philadelphus* Virginal.
Opposite top: Another white-flowered gem – *Rubus* Tridel.

spellbinding effect of white flowers.

A patch of white is extraordinarily effective since it captures and reflects light. To a dark day it will bring brightness, to a hot day it will add a touch of cool. At dawn it will be the first place to signal the beginning of the day, at dusk it will be the last to disappear into the gloom. And it will play particularly exciting optical tricks beneath trees, where it will give an illusion of light when there is none.

My first white planting was in a woodland garden, a dark and mysterious place which the sun barely penetrated. Here I persuaded the white form of *Clematis montana* to grow up the overhanging trees and wreathe among their branches. Beneath them I planted some of the Himalayan bramble, *Rubus biflorus*, which throws up beautiful white stems each year when the old growth has been cut away. And I found room for several white-flowering rhododendrons and azaleas.

For ground cover I used both the wild wood anemones which wandered in of their own accord from beyond the fence, and the charming little woodruff, *Asperula odorata*. I planted great clumps of fragrant lily of the valley, and, of course, I included hundreds of bulbs, mainly snowdrops – but also

Opposite: Perhaps the most beautiful white garden of all – the one at Sissinghurst created by Victoria Sackville-West.

the less well-known spring snowflake, *Leucojum vernum* – white *Muscari botryoides album*, hyacinths and several varieties of white narcissi.

My woodland corner looked beautiful always, at any time of day, at any season of the year. But in winter moonlight it took on an ethereal quality all its own. I loved it dearly.

But white flowers don't have to be planted against trees to look effective. It's perfectly acceptable either to set aside part of the border for them, or to use an island bed surrounded by lawn. For minimum care concentrate on perennials and bulbs for the most part, but use annuals and bedding plants to fill any gaps.

If your chosen site is sunny instead of shady there are many more flowers to choose from including old favourites of the herbaceous border. For instance, there are white foxgloves and fox-tail lilies (*Eremurus robustus*), peonies and petunias, dianthus and delphiniums, as well as marguerites and Michaelmas daisies, chrysanthemums and Canterbury bells. And there are good white astilbes, aquilegias, arabis and alyssum, pyrethrums, primulas, pansies and even poppies – the list is endless.

In the centre of a white island, or towards the back of a border, you could use bean poles to make a fountain of white sweet peas. Or you could create height by planting a superb white rose. I would make my choice from among *alba maxima*, the Jacobite rose, Mme Hardy with its suggestion of lemon fragrance, Prosperity and Blanc Double de Coubert. If you would prefer a different sort of shrub rather than a rose you could use the popular mock orange, *Philadelphus* Virginal or, better still, Beauclerk. Or what about *Rubus* Tridel, another handsome bramble, with delicate arching shoots and large rose-like flowers? I think the splendid rubus family are greatly undervalued by gardeners at present, and can't imagine why they aren't more popular. They are easy to grow, and among them produce some lovely fruits, stems and flowers.

For subtle contrasts and textures in your white garden intersperse your flowers and shrubs with some of the silver-leaved plants which make such a superb foil for them. I would recommend four in particular.

Artemisia Lambrook Silver is especially valuable. It makes a lovely border plant; it can be used in flower arrangements, either freshly cut or hung and dried; and its rather odd smell is a fly repellent. One minor problem – its smell repels me too and I prefer not to use it indoors.

Senecio laxifolius is another flower arranger's favourite, a good, sturdy, low-growing shrub with white stems and abundant, golden, daisy-like flowers from midsummer. If it is cut back each spring it stays neat and shapely and its white-edged leaves are always fresh and bright.

Santolina chamaecyparissus is a good little silver bush with lovely aromatic foliage and yellow flowers. Again, it needs a spring trim if it's to keep its figure and complexion.

Finally, *Stachys* Silver Carpet is a splendid pale, weed-smother, ground-cover plant which looks very good in the white garden or beneath roses in a mixed border.

Incidentally, all of these are at their best in hot, dry, sunny conditions. Too much shade or damp and, like Cinderella at midnight, their silver sheen turns drab and dirty.

Again, finish off your white garden with some of the host of white-flowered bulbs that are available, not only those that do well in the shade, but also the sun-lovers like tulips and crocuses which will open out wide their glistening cups to drink in every drop of early sunshine.

A final thought for a white garden: you could have a formal bed of pure white floribunda roses rising from a blue mist of forget-me-nots. Iceberg is still my favourite white floribunda, but there are other good ones, particularly Ice White, and the vigorous old French lady, Yvonne Rabier.

Whichever form of white garden you choose, one thing is certain. A cool and restful place you will find it, and you'll return to it again and again for the tranquil pleasure it will give you.

The Labour~free Garden ~ a final thought

Throughout the book I've been concentrating on a complete family garden with a full range of shrubs, flowers, fruit, herbs and vegetables which can be grown without too much work. The main method of saving labour has been through the careful choice of plants – selecting perennials wherever possible, growing dwarf varieties to eliminate staking, choosing hardy varieties that can look after themselves and don't succumb too easily to climatic

conditions or disease, preferring roses and fruit that don't need much pruning, bush tomatoes that don't have to be tied up or pinched out, and so on.

We've also decided to let nature be its own doctor by using herbs as insecticides and fertilisers so that we don't have to spend expensive hours with a kill-and-cure spray.

And we've relegated time-consumers like alpines to a very minor role.

However, these decisions are all labour-saving. They are not labour-*eliminating*.

The only garden that doesn't need work is a concrete yard. And even then it would have to be sprayed with weed-killer at regular intervals to annihilate those brave seedlings that would still persist in putting down their roots in any square inch of dust they could find.

Still, if you really have neither time nor inclination for gardening, or if your garden is merely a week-end retreat and you have other things to do with your leisure than labour in it, there *is* an easy way out.

Design yourself a chequer-board garden. Level off the ground, or terrace it if it slopes, then pave most of it – but leave a few gaps – using a combination of plain and coloured paving stones to make it as light and bright as possible. Concrete the majority of the stones into place but leave a few loose so that they can be easily lifted and the space used for short-term planting. A square of annuals, perhaps, or a courgette, a cucumber plant or dwarf tomato could spend the summer here, and the slabs replaced after they have flowered or fruited.

In the permanent spaces put plants which need minimum care. A group of sturdy shrubs, chosen for variety of height, shape and flowering period, will give some colour and greenery all year round. Other soil-squares could house prostrate herbs – thymes in particular – or a tiny collection of alpines. Yet another could take a small tree underplanted with bulbs. One or two gaps left by fencing, or near the walls of the house, should be used for sturdy climbers to give that vital extra

dimension. The choice and placing depend entirely on your personal preference, soil and situation.

If and when you feel strong enough you could add some flowering troughs and tubs, window boxes and hanging baskets to give extra colour and interest, or even sink into the paving an ornamental lily pond.

The effect will be elegant – and it couldn't possibly be simpler.

Opposite: A courtyard with containers and a pool. The use of plants with sculptural foliage suits the formal setting.
Below: A small town garden simply created by removing the odd paving slab.

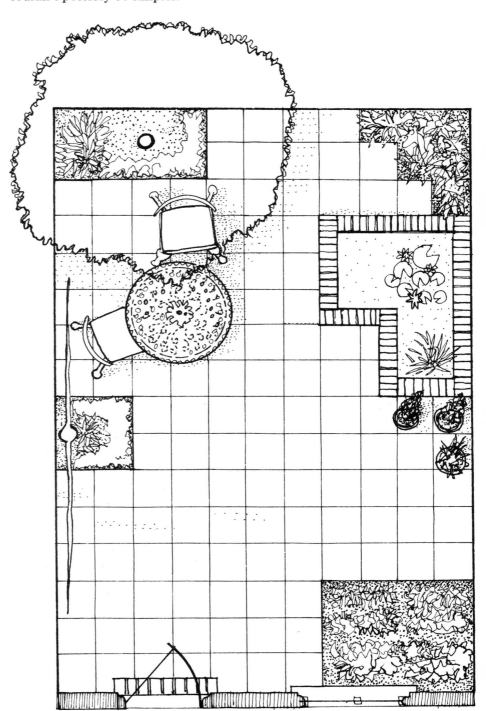

Index

Page numbers in italics denote illustrations

Acer palmatum dissectum 68
Aconite 20, 116
African Marigold 82
Agapanthus 97
Ajuga 66
Allium 20, 97
    pest control by 101
Allspice 112
alpines 121
    for small garden 70
aluminium lawn edging 34, *34*
Alyssum 45, 118
    Royal Carpet 111
    saxatile (yellow) 24, 109
    Snow Carpet 111
Anemone 20
    blanda 97, 116
    nemorosa (Wood Anemone) 117
annuals 121
    for containers 75
    hardy: for quick colour 66
Anthemis (Chamomile):
    benefit to other plants 82
    nobilis 112
    tea 82
Antirrhinum 104
    games with 46
ants: herbs to discourage 82
aphids: natural control of 101
Apothecary's Rose 96
Apple trees 93
    espalier: pruning *93*
    in lawn 36
Aquilegia 118
Arabis 24, 118
Armeria caespitosa 57
Artemisia arborescens 97
    Lambrook Silver 118
Asparagus: herbs of benefit to 82
Asparagus Peas 72, 85, *85*
Asperula odorata 20, 117
Astilbe 22, 118
Aubrieta 77, 109
awnings 25, *25*
Azalea 19, 117

Baby Blue Eyes 45
Bacon, Francis 112
ball games 52
Balm 81, 112
    tea 82
barbecue:
    permanent: building 48, *49*
    portable *32–3*
    tending *48*
barrow 12
    child playing with 12, *13*
Basil 81
    benefit to other plants 82
    as insecticide 82
Bay leaves 80, 112
Bay tree 72, *72*
Beans, Broad 47
Beans, French 47, 72, 86, *86*
    freezing 86
    salting 86
Beans, Runner 72, 86
    freezing 86
    salting 86
beauty care: herbs for 82
bedding plants, summer: for
    containers 75
beds:
    planting 65

raised 54, *55*
    tiered *71*
Begonia 76
Berberis 19, *105*
    darwinii 104
    stenophylla 114
    wilsoniae 104
Bergamot 22, 112
    tea 82
Betula pendula youngii 115
Birch: weeping 115
bird bath 107, *107*
bird pudding 104
birds *102–3*, 104–7
    feeding 104
    keeping off seeded lawn 64–5
    keeping off seedlings 82
    plants to grow for 104
Bird's Foot Trefoil 108
bird table 107, *107*
Blackberries 52, 92
    leaves: tisane 82
black spot: natural control of 101
Bladder Campion *16–17*
    conditions found in 16
bog garden 22–3
    creating in dry garden 22–4
    cross-section *22*
Borage:
    benefit to other plants 82
    candied 82
    eating 99
borders:
    easy-care 36
    mixed 97
    planting 65
bounce-back 52, *52–3*
bouquets garnis 80
Bramble, *see* Rubus
Broom 19, 25, 108
    Moroccan 111
Buddleia 19, 108
    alternifolia 108
    davidii nanhoensis 108
bulbs:
    for containers 75
    easy-care 37
    in hanging basket 76
    in mixed border 97
    for small garden 70
    for white garden 117–18
Burnet 112
Burnet Rose 25
butter:
    herb 82, *83*
    rose 99
Buttercup *16–17*
    conditions found in 16
Butterflies: plants to attract 17, 108–9
Butterfly Bush, *see* Buddleia

Cabbage: herbs of benefit to 82
cabbage root fly 108
Calendula 45, 66
    officinalis: culinary uses 82
    Radio 45
Californian Poppy 66
Callitriche verna 51
Caltha palustris 22
Camellia japonica 22
Campanula *16–17*, 19, 57
    medium (Canterbury Bells) 118
    soil found in 16
Candytuft (Iberis) 25, 45
Canterbury Bells 118
Carnation 111
caterpillars: food for 17
cats: keeping away from sandpits 40
cavy 42
Centaurea:
    cyanus (Cornflower) *16–17*, 45, 66
    conditions found in 16
    moschata 111
Centranthus ruber 108
chalk: plants liking *19*

chalk soil:
    plants for 19–20
    treatment 19
Chamaecyparis:
    lawsoniana erecta 115
    Green Hedger 63
    obtusa nana 57
Chamomile 112
    benefit to other plants 82
    tea 82
Charlock 108
chequerboard garden 121, *121*
Cherry:
    ornamental 68
    winter 114
Cherry Pie 112
children:
    encouraging to work in garden 44–5
    young: garden to play in 28–9,
        38–47, *38*
Chimonanthus praecox 114
    p. lutens 111
China Aster 104
Chionodoxa 57, 116
Chives 81
    pest control by 101
Christmas Rose 116
Chrysanthemum 20, 118
Cistus 25
clay:
    acidity 18
    plants for 19
    treatment 18
Clematis 19, *73*
    growing on other plants 73
    montana 20, 72, *116*, 117
    tanguitca 72
climbers 121
    for small garden 72–3
climbing frame 40, *41*
clothing 12–13
Clover *16–17*
    benefits of 17
    conditions found in 16
Cloves 112
club root 108
Cobri Peas 85
colour: use of 77
Coltsfoot *16–17*
    benefits of 17
    conditions found in 16
Complete Herbal (Culpeper) 98
conservatory 15, 59
    other uses 69
containers:
    at different levels 76
    for old or handicapped 54
    planted up *75*
    planting 74
    plants for 75
    selection 74
    for small garden 70, 74–7
Cornflower *16–17*, 45, 66
    conditions found in 16
Cornus 19
    alba sibirica 115
    stolonifera flaviramea 115
Cosmos 104
Cotoneaster 104
    conspicuus 114
    hybridus pendulus 114
Couch Grass 82
Courgette 72, 87, *87*, 121
Cranesbill 25
Creeping Jenny, *see* Lysimachia
Crocus 116, 118
    species 57, 97
croquet 52, *52–3*
cucumber 72, 89, 121
    braised (recipe) 89
Culpeper, Nicholas 98
Cupressocyparis leylandii 63
Cypress 72
Cytisus battandieri 111

Daffodil, *see* Narcissus
Daisy *16–17*
    benefits of 17
    conditions found in 16
    making 'grandma-in-a-bonnet' 46,
        46
damp area: making into bog garden 22
Dandelion *16–17*
    benefits of 17
    conditions found in 16
Daphne mezereum 22, 111, 114
Day Lily 22
Delphinium 118
Deutzia 19
Dianthus 19, 57, 118. See also
    Carnation, Pink
Dicentra 22
Diervilla 19
digging: single *18*
Dog's Tooth Violet 20
Dog Violet 108
dolly: making from Poppy 46, *46*
drought: plants surviving in 24–5
Dryas octopetala 57
Dusty Miller, *see Primula auricula*

eating outdoors *50*
electricity: taking lead outdoors 14–15
Epimedium 22
Eremurus robustus 118
Erica carnea 116
    darleyensis 116
Erythronium dens-canis 20
Escallonia 25
Eschscholzia 66
Euphorbia palustris 22
Evening Primrose 104

fences: climbers for 36, 37, 66
Fennel 81
    drying 80
ferns 22
fertiliser, natural 101
fish 51
flies: repellants for 82, 118
Flowering Currant 19
flowers: games with 46
flower show: children staging *43*
football goal-posts 52, *52–3*
Forget-me-not 118
    Water 22
Forsythia 22, 73
Foxglove 118
Fox-tail Lily 118
fragrance, *see* scent
freckles: treatment for 82
Fritillaria meleagris 20
fruit 90–3
fruit bushes 52
fruit salad with rose petals 100
fruit trees: in small garden 72
Fuchsia 76, 97
furniture, garden 14, *32–3*

games:
    for garden 52, *52–3*
    with flowers 46
Garlic 81
    pest control by 82, 101
Garrya elliptica 114
gazebo 58
Gentiana sino-ornata 116
Geranium:
    (Cranesbill) 25
    (Pelargonium) 76
gloves 13
goal-posts 52, *52–3*
goldfish 51
Gooseberries 92
    pruning *92*
gooseberry sawfly 92
Gorse 108
'grab': for picking up refuse 61, *61*
'grandma-in-a-bonnet' 46, *46*
grass: importance of 34

greenfly: natural control of 101
greenhouse:
  automatic 58, *58*
  other uses 69, *69*
  siting 63
ground cover 64, 117–18
  easy-care, grow-anywhere 37
Ground Elder 82
Ground Ivy 82
Groundsel *16–17*
  conditions found in 16
growing-bag 76
growing old: garden plan for *28–9*,
  54, 54–61
growing up: garden plan for *28–9*,
  48, 48–53
guinea pig 42

hair care: herbs for 82
Hamamelis mollis 111, 114
hammocks *36*
hanging baskets 76
  planting 76, *76*
Hart's-tongue Fern 22
headaches: cures for 98, 112
Heather 19, 108
hedgehog 41, *42*
Hedge Mustard 108
hedges:
  easy-care 37
  Roses for 97
Helianthemum 25
Helianthus (Sunflower) *annuus* 45
  seeds 104
Heliotrope 112
Helleborus corsicus 115
  niger 116
Hemerocallis 22
herbaceous plants: in mixed border 97
herb garden 31, 80–2
  planting 80
  siting 63, 80
herbs:
  benefits to other plants 82
  butter (recipe) 82, *83*
  carpeting 112
  in container 72, 80
  culinary uses 82
  drying 80
  freezing 80
  in hanging basket 76
  in knot garden 112, *112–13*
  pillow of 112
  prostrate 121
  for small garden 70
  for starter garden 37
  teas 82
Hesperis 108–9
Himalayan Bramble, *see Rubus biflorus*
Himalayan Cowslip, *see Primula*
  florindae
Himalayan Poppy 22
hoe, automatic 61, *61*
Holly, *see* Ilex
Hollyhock: making lady from flower
  46
Honesty 46, 116
Honeysuckle, *see* Lonicera
Horsechestnut tree 68
Horsetail *16–17*, 82
  conditions found in 16
Hosta 21, *21*, 97
  crispula undulata 21
  fortunei albopicta 21
  plantaginea 21
  sieboldiana 21
hot, dry garden: plants for 24–5
Hottonia 51
Houseleek, *see* Sempervivum
Hyacinth 111, 118
Hydrangea petiolaris 73
Hypericum calycinum 109
hypertufa 55
Hyssop 112

Iberis (Candytuft) 25, 45
ice on pool: melting 51
Ilex (Holly) *106*, 114
  Golden King 104, *114*
  Madame Briot 104
insecticides:
  herbs as 82
  plants as 100–1
instant garden 66
Iris histrioides 57, 111, 116
  kaempferi 22
  reticulata 57, 97, 111, 116
  sibirica 22
  unguicularis 116
Ivy 76

Jacobite Rose 118
Jasmine, *see* Jasminum
Jasminum nudiflorum 22, 73, 114
  officinale 111
Juniper, *see* Juniperus
Juniperus 72
  communis compressa 57
  hibernica 115

Kingcup 22
kitchen garden 31, 84–93
  site 63, 84
  starting 65
kneeler *60*, 61
knees: protection for 13
Kniphofia 67
knot garden 112, *112–13*

labour-free garden 120–1
Laburnum 68
Lamium 66
Lavender 25, 112
  as insecticide 82
lawn:
  altering shape 69
  aluminium edging 34, *34*
  flexibility of 34
  mowing 34
  from seed *35*, 64–5
  specimen tree in 36, *65*
  stepping stones for children's
    traffic 41
  from turf 34, *35*, 64
Lawson's Cypress 63, 115
Leptosiphon 45
Lettuce 47, 89, *89*
  Buttercrunch 89
  Salad Bowl 89
  soup (recipe) 89
  Suzan 89
  Tom Thumb 72
Leucojum vernum 118
Leyland Cypress 63
lighting for patio *32–3*
Lilac 111
Lilium auratum 112
  regale 22, 112
Lily of the Valley 111, 117
lime:
  plants disliking 19
  plants liking 19–20, *19*
linen: scenting 20
Livingstone Daisy
  (Mesembryanthemum) 24, *25*
Lobelia 76
London Pride 20
Lonicera (Honeysuckle) 15, 20, 37, 104
  americana 66
  fragrantissima 112, 114
  japonica halliana 66, 72–3, 110, 112
Lupinus arboreus 25
Lysimachia nummularia 66, 107

Magnolia 19
Mahonia japonica 114
Maple, Japanese 68
Marguerite 118
Marigold 66
  African 82

benefit to other plants 82
  culinary uses 99
  pot: culinary uses 82
  Scotch 45
Marjoram 80, 81, 112
Marvel of Peru 112
Mayweed *16–17*
  conditions found in 16
Meconopsis betonicifolia 22
Melissa officinalis (Balm) 81, 112
  tea 82
Mentha pulegium 112
  requienii 112
Mesembryanthemum 24, *25*
Michaelmas Daisy 20, 109, 118
mildew: natural control of 101
Mimulus 22
Mints 80, 81, 112
  benefit to other plants 82
  drying 80
  as fly repellant 82
  as insecticide 82
Mirabilis 112
mirrors: in garden 77
Mock Orange, *see* Philadelphus
Moluccella 116
Monarda didyma (Bergamot) 22, 112
  tea 82
Moroccan Broom 111
Mountain Ash, *see Sorbus aucuparia*
mouse: death of 44–5
mower 34, 61
Muscari 97, 116
  botryoides album 111, 118
Myosotis (forget-me-not) 118
  palustris 22
Myrrhis odorata 112

Narcissus (incl. Daffodil) 118
  Angel's Tears 57
  dwarf 116
  Hoop Petticoat 57
  Jonquil 111
  pheasant's eye 111
Nasturtium 45, 76
  eating 45, 99
  growing up trees 73
Nemesia 45
Nemophila 45
Nettle, Stinging 108
  benefits of 17
  as natural fertiliser 101
new garden 63–6
  planning 63
  preparing 63
Nicotiana 24
  affinis 112
Night-scented Stock 112
Noah's Ark Juniper 57
nursery garden *28–9*, 38–47, *38*

Oenothera 104
old people: garden for *28–9*, *54*, 54–61
Onion family: use for pest control 101
Origanum onites (Marjoram) 80, 81,
  112
Osmunda 22
Oxalis adenophylla 57

Pansy 118
  making 'man in the chair' 46
Papaver (Poppy) 118
  making dolly from 46, *46*
  orientale (Oriental Poppy) 24, 116
  rhoeas 66
Parsley 37, 80
  in beauty care 82
  benefit to other plants 82
  drying 80
  pest control by 101
paths:
  giving illusion of space 77

making 64, *65*
  types *64*
patio 30–1, *30*, *31*
  making 64, 69
paved garden *73*, *120*, 121, *121*
Pear, Willow-leaved, *see Pyrus*
  salicifolius
Pear trees 93
Peas 47, 85
peat bed: making 20
Pelargonium (Geranium) 76
  scented-leaved 111, 112
peninsula, flower: easy-care 36
Penstemon 20
Peony 97, 118
Peppermint: in tisane 82
perennials:
  easy-care 37
  planting 65
  for small gardens 70
  transplanting 69
pergola: making greenhouse into 69
Periwinkle 20
Pernettya 19
  mucronata 115
pests: plants to control 82, 100–1
petits pois 85
pets 41–2
Petunia 24, 76, 118
Philadelphus 19, 97, *117*
  Beauclerk 118
  coronarius 110
  Virginal 118
Phlox 57, 111
Phyllitis 22
Physalis 116
'physician plant' 82
pillow, herb 112
Pink 77, 111
planning 14–15, *28–61*
  garden for growing old *28–9*, *54*,
    54–61
  garden for growing up *28–9*, *48*,
    48–53
  new garden 63
  nursery garden *28–9*, 38–47, *38*
  starter garden *28–9*, 30–7, *30*
Plantain *16–17*
  conditions found in 16
Plantain Lily, *see* Hosta
Polygonum baldschuanicum 42, 66
pool:
  dangers with young children 40
  ice on 51
  inflatable *38*, 40
  small *51*
  turning sandpit into 48–9
  using as sandpit 39
Poppy 118
  making dolly from 46, *46*
  Oriental 24, 116
  Shirley 66
Potatoes 46–7, 84
  herbs of benefit to 82
  salad (recipe) 84
  storing 84
Potentilla 25
pot-pourri 112
Primrose 20
Primula 19, 20, 118
  auricula 22, 111
  candelabra types 22
  florindae 22
  vulgaris (Primrose) 20
problem gardens: coming to terms
  with 15
Prunus (Cherry) 68
  subhirtella autumnalis rosea 114
Pyracantha 115
Pyrethrum 118
pyrethrum (insecticide) 107
Pyrus salicifolius 66, 68

rabbits *40*, 41
Radish Sparkler 47

raised beds 54, *55*
Raspberries 52, 92
  leaves: tisane 82
  Zeva: in containers 72, 92
rats: herbs to keep away 82
Red-hot Pokers 67
Rhododendron 19, 20, 117
Rhubarb 72, 93
Ribes 19
Rosa (Rose) 72, 94–101, *98–9*, 111
  alba 96
    maxima 118
  Albéric Barbier 96
  Albertine 96
  Amy Robsart 97
  Baron Girod de l'Ain 97
  Blanc Double de Coubert 118
  Boule de Neige 97
  bourbons 97
  Buff Beauty 96
  Canary Bird 96
  candied 82, 99
  Céleste 96
  centifolias 97
  climbers 15, 94, 96
    pruning 97
  Cornelia 97
  culinary uses 99–100
  Etoile de Hollande 96, 99
  Felicia 97
  floribunda 118
  Fountain 96
  fruit salad with Rose petals
    (recipe) 100
  gallica 98
    officinalis 96
  growing Clematis on 73
  growing on trees 73
  as hedge 97
  hips 96
  hybrid perpetuals 97
  Iceberg 118
  Ice White 118
  Madame Hardy 118
  Maiden's Blush 97
  medical properties 98
  Meg Merrilies 97
  in mixed border 97
  Moonlight 96
  moyesii 96
    Geranium 115
  mundi 95, 97
  Nevada *100*
  New Dawn 96
  Penelope 97
  pest control by neighbouring
    plants 100–1
  petals: candied 92, 99
    conserve (recipe) 99
    pot-pourri 112
  Petite de Hollande 97
  planting *101*
  Prosperity 118
  ramblers 94, 96
    pruning 97
  Sanders' White 96
  Sharbatee Gulab (recipe) 100
  shrub 96–7
  spinosissima 25
  standard: in pot 72
  Thisbe 96
  vinegar (recipe) 98
  white 118
  Yvonne Rabier 118
  Zéphirine Drouhin *94*, 96
Rose, *see* Rosa
Rosemary 25, 81, 112
  in beauty care 82
  benefit to other plants 82
  candied 82
  as insecticide 82
  tea 82
Rose of Sharon 109
rotary-drier 42–3, *42*

roundabout 40
Rowan, *see Sorbus aucuparia*
Royal Fern 22
Rubus biflorus 117
  Tridel *117*, 118
Russian Vine 42, 66

Sackville-West, Victoria 116
Sage 81
  in beauty care 82
  benefit to other plants 82
  as insecticide 82
sandpit 39, *39*
  keeping cats away from 40
  turning into pool 48–9
sandwiches:
  Nasturtium 45
  Rose petal 99
Sanguisorba 112
Santolina 97
  chamaecyparissus 112
Saponaria 25, 57
Saxifraga (Saxifrage) 57
  umbrosa 20
Scabious 19, 104, 109
Scarlet Pimpernel *16–17*
  conditions found in 16
scent:
  garden for 63, 110–13
  positioning plants for 110
  through the year 110–12
Scilla 20, 116
Scotch Brier 25
Scotch Marigold 45
screen, moveable *14*, 15, 25
secateurs 61, *61*
second-hand garden 67–9
Sedum 24, 109
Sempervivum 24, 57
Senecio chamaecyparissus 118
  laxifolius 24, 25
shade:
  of buildings: plants for 21–2
  cool garden in *23*
  providing 25
  of trees: heavy, plants for 20
    light, plants for 20–1
Sharbatee Gulab 100
shed 42, *69*
  other uses 69
Shepherd's Purse *16–17*
  conditions found in 16
shoes 12–13
shrubs:
  for containers 75
  easy-care 37
  planting 65
  for small garden 70
  transplanting 69
Sissinghurst: White Garden 116, *119*
Skimmia 115
skin care 82, 98
sleep: inducing 98
small garden 63, 70–9, *71*, *73*
  plants for 70–3, 78–9
  rules 70
Snake's-head Fritillary 20
Snapdragon, *see* Antirrhinum
Snowdrop 20, 97, 115, 116, 117
Snowflake 118
soil:
  chalk: plants liking *19*, 19–20
    treatment 19
  clay: acidity 18
    plants for 19
    treatment 18
  deficiencies improved by weeds
    16–17
  judging type by weeds 16
  testing *15*, 15–16
Sorrel, mint 82
Sorbus aucuparia (Mountain Ash,
    Rowan) 104, *104*
  a. aspleniifolia 115
Sorrel *16–17*, 108

benefits of 17
  conditions found in 16
soup: lettuce (recipe) 89
space: illusion of 77
spade: for elderly 61, *61*
Spiraea 19
Spurrey *16–17*
  conditions found in 16
Stachys Silver Carpet 97, 118
starter garden: plan *28–9*, 30–7, *30*
stepping stones in lawn: for
    children's traffic 41
Stocks 111
Stonecrop, *see* Sedum
Strawberries 90–1, *91*
  alpine 72, 91
  in containers 72
  cup (recipe) 91
  growing in barrel 90–1, *90*
  herbs of benefit to 82
  leaves: in tisane 82
Sugar Peas 85
summerhouse 58
sun: plants for 24–5
sunblinds 25, *25*
Sunflower 45
  seeds 104
Sweet Cicely 112
Sweet Peas 111, 118
Sweet Rocket 108–9
Sweet Sultan 111
swing 40, *41*
symbiosis 100–1

Tagetes erecta 82
teas, herb 82
tennis: with anchored ball 52, *52–3*
terrace 30–1, *30*, *31*
Thistle 108
  benefits of 17
Thrift 77
Thuja plicata semperaurescens 115
Thyme, *see* Thymus
Thymus (Thyme) 25, 57, 80, 81, 107,
    121
  in beauty care 82
  benefit to other plants 82
  lemon-scented 112
  serpyllum 112
  in tisane 82
tisanes 82
Tobacco Plant 24, 112
Tomatoes 88, *88*, 121
  in containers 72
  creamed (recipe) 88
  herbs of benefit to 82
tools 12, *12–13*
  for elderly 61, *61*
toys, garden 40–1
Tree Lupin 25
trees:
  in containers 72
  plants in tubs or paving under 20, *21*
  positioning 68
  silhouettes 67
  for small gardens 70
  specimen, in lawn 36, 65
  too large 68
  transplanting 69
trough garden:
  making 54–7, *56–7*
  plants for 57
trowel, long-handled 61, *61*
Tulip 118
Turnip 47, 87
turnip flea beetle 108
tyre: for games 52, *52–3*

umbrella for shade 25
utilities 42–3

Valerian 108
vegetables 84–9
  for children 46–7
  in small garden 72

for starter garden 37
Verbena 76
Veronica 109
Vetch *16–17*
  benefits of 17
  conditions found in 16
Viburnum 112
  fragrans 22, 111, 114
Vinca 20
vinegar: Rose (recipe) 98
Viola 57
  canina (Dog Violet) 108
  odorata (Violet) 111
  Pansy 118
    making 'man in the chair' 46
Violet 111

Wallflower 77, 111
walls:
  hollow 54
  plants for 66
  pots on 76–7, *77*
washing-line, rotary 42–3, *42*
Water Forget-me-not 22
watering: making easy 59
Water Lily: planting 51, *51*
Water-mints 112
Water Starwort 51
Water Violet 51
weedkillers: plants acting as 82
weeds:
  chart *16–17*
  judging soil type by 16
  soil deficiencies improved by 16–17
Wendy house 40, *41*
wheelbarrow 12
  child playing in 12, *13*
wheelchair:
  adapting garden to take 58
  gardening for people in 54, *54*
white garden 116–18, *119*
wild garden 20–1
winter garden 63, 114–16
Winter Sweet 111, 114
Wisteria 19
  growing on trees 73
Witch Hazel 111, 114
Wood Anemone 117
woodland garden 20–1, 117–18
Woodruff 20, 117
working outdoors 15

Yellow Rocket 108